NO MAN'S LAND

First published in 2007 by
Liberties Press
Guinness Enterprise Centre | Taylor's Lane | Dublin 8 | Ireland
www.LibertiesPress.com
General and sales enquiries: +353 (1) 415 1224 | peter@libertiespress.com
Editorial: +353 (1) 415 1287 | sean@libertiespress.com

Trade enquiries to CMD Distribution
55A Spruce Avenue | Stillorgan Industrial Park | Blackrock | County Dublin
Tel: +353 (1) 294 2560 | Fax: +353 (1) 294 2564

Distributed in the United States by
Dufour Editions
PO Box 7 | Chester Springs | Pennsylvania | 19425

and in Australia by
James Bennett Pty Limited | InBooks
3 Narabang Way | Belrose NSW 2085

Liberties Press is a member of Clé,
the Irish Book Publishers' Association.

ISBN: 978–1–905483–26–6

2 4 6 8 10 9 7 5 3 1

A CIP record for this title is available from the British Library.

Set in Garamond
Printed in Ireland by ßetaprint
Bluebell Industrial Estate | Dublin 12 | Ireland.

No Man's Land

Dispatches from the Middle East

Richard Crowley

For my mother and father

CONTENTS

This land. This land is no man's land.
God made this world. This land don't belong to one man.
You gotta die one day. Leave it all behind.
You oughta be ashamed. Fighting over your burial ground.

John Lee Hooker, 'This World'

PREFACE

There is no excuse for not knowing what's happening in Israel and the Palestinian Territories. All the necessary information is easily accessible. In terms of news coverage, the major media outlets make the Israeli-Palestinian conflict one of the most frequently reported conflicts on the agenda. At times of crisis, there are more journalists here than in any other place in the world, except for Washington. Foreign governments place some of the best people in their embassies here to find out what's going on. It seems that every parliment in the world has sent a cross-party delegation to the region on a fact-finding mission. All the top human-rights groups are represented here, and are constantly producing comprehensive reports on the causes and effects of this conflict. But if the international community understands the backround, why can it not come up with a workable solution? I believe it is because there has been no genuine, sustained effort by the outside world to come up with a plan and make it work. For reasons of its own, the international community has repeatedly failed to act with the determination and the impartiality needed to settle this conflict.

To a large extent, the international community dragged the Israelis and the Palestinians into this mess. Now they have an undeniable responsibility to help get them out of it. In the 1930s and 40s, the British colonial masters of Palestine made promises to both the Jewish and Arab populations that could not be kept. When it became apparent that the competing claims of the two communities were leading inexorably to war, the British government attempted to pass the problem on to the United Nations. The UN, given the unenviable task of dividing the land up between Arab and Jew, came up with a line on the map which inevitably provoked the hostilities that continue to this day. It is now up to the UN to come up with a new map, based on the new realities and the changed attitudes of those who are affected.

The UN is part of the Middle East Quartet, which also includes the United States, the EU and Russia. The Quartet has the political and economic clout to insist to the Israelis and the Palestinians that this fight has to end soon. If the international community acts with determination and, above all, impartiality, the Quartet can play a valuable role in securing peace. It can suggest a new framework, but it must also use its strength to force the two sides to engage in negotiations which could lead to a lasting peace deal. This will not be easy. The Quartet is beset by divisions and rivalry, and a lethargy brought on by countless previous failed attempts to resolve the conflict. But with considerably less effort, and for far less cost than the current intervention in Iraq, the international community could help the two sides achieve a fair and durable solution to this problem.

The world ignores this conflict at its peril. The fighting between the Israelis and the Palestinians has the potential to ignite a full-scale war. Locally, it acts as a provocation for bitter armed struggle. In the region as a whole, the fighting creates tremors which are felt not only in Beirut but also in Cairo,

Amman and Damascus. The Middle East is no longer the arena for a proxy war between East and West, but it has increasingly become the battleground for the extremists of Islam and their Western enemies. On either side, the fight has been taken up by some very dangerous new players. The honourable cause of Palestinian independence and statehood has been hijacked, and used to fuel a sinister new anti-Semitism and a grotesque international jihad against the West. The defence of the State of Israel is a rallying call for the shady neo-con forces who wield a dangerously disproportionate share of power in the United States.

These outside influences have tightened the knots which bind the Palestinians and the Israelis. On one side, the Palestinians have become more and more alienated from the international community, including the supposedly representative Arab League. The stifling grip of the occupation, and the infuriating indignity which it brings, the poverty which it causes and, above all, the anger which Palestinians feel about the clear injustices which are heaped upon them, has resulted in a hardening of attitudes that will be difficult to reverse. At the same time, the Jewish people's justifiable fears of another genocide, and their legitimate need to live peacefully in the region, have been played upon and distorted by the extremists among them to try to justify further territorial expansion and a policy of belligerent and often brutal occupation of the Palestinian territories.

This latest phase of the conflict has resulted in massive civilian deaths. Thousands of people have been killed, tens of thousands have been horribly injured and maimed, and the psychological damage that has been inflicted on the two peoples has yet to be understood. I once met a seven-year-old Palestinian child in Bethlehem who went to bed each night with his socks and shoes on so that he could run from the Israeli soldiers who chased him every night in his dreams. A teenage

Israeli girl tried to kill herself by throwing herself out of a high-rise apartment block. She felt guilty because her best friend had been killed by a suicide bomber outside a nightclub, and she had not. There are thousands of stories like those, and there are tens of thousands of people who know only fear and suspicion. The vast majority on either side express little hope of a compromise. They have begun to believe that the situation has gone too far. Indeed, most commentators, whatever their beliefs, now agree that the time to find a just solution to the Israeli-Palestinian conflict is fast running out. If agreement is not reached within a matter of a few years, the situation will have deteriorated to such an extent that it will be virutally impossible to make peace for perhaps a generation or more.

The majority on either side say that they are prepared to make peace. But their prescription for how that can be achieved varies widely. The differences are not just between the two communities but also *within* the two communities. Unless and until the Palestinians and the Israelis agree among themselves what it is they are prepared to relinquish in order to achieve peace, there can be no real negotiations between the two sides. In the future, there may be fresh initiatives and peace conferences, and even some new deals signed. However, without a new and explicit declaration by a clear majority of both Israelis and Palestinians that they genuinely accept the notion of a two-state solution, based on a framework to be negotiated by the two sides as real equals, there will no end to this war.

*

I would like to thank all of the people who made it possible for me to write this book. But I would not have done it, nor *could* I have done it, had I not spent more than three years living and working here as RTÉ's correspondent in the region. Many thanks, therefore, to Director of News Ed Mulhall, and to RTÉ's editorial, technical and administrative staff.

I owe a huge debt of gratitude to the many Palestinians and Israelis who helped me do my job during my frequent stays here since 2001. They were doing their job too. But some of them did more than that. They went out of their way to make me feel genuinely welcomed. People like Hiyan and Sausan, Labeeb and Tahrier, Sammy and Ariela, Meir, Mark, Akram, Danny, Ami and Anat, Uri and another Ami, Michal and Tom, three Ahmads and two Mohammads, and numerous other good people in Jerusalem, Gaza, Tel Aviv and Ramallah. These people are not 'contacts'; I count them as friends and deeply appreciate their kindness and hospitality.

A word of thanks, too, to the ex-pat community, the fellow foreigners living here who offered unbiased explanations, real camraderie and strong alcohol to keep me going. Thanks to Graham, Roz, Ray, Sean, Margaret, Isolde, Colm, Pat, Niall, Alan, Eoin, Joanne, Philip, Maeve, Paul, Michael, Ferry, Nuala and Ed. I owe them all a drink. Those I have neglected to mention are owed two drinks.

In particular, I would like to thank the people who agreed to be interviewed at length for the book. I greatly appreciate their time and their honesty. A few of them wished to have their names changed; I reluctantly agreed, on the basis that this allowed them speak freely.

Many thanks to Seán and Peter at Liberties Press for their patience and understanding, and a special thanks to Khaled Zighari, the Jerusalem photographer who supplied the image for the cover. Finally, a very special thank-you to Aoife Kavanagh. This book would not have been written without her support.

Richard Crowley, Jerusalem, 2007

INTRODUCTION

If there is any spark of life remaining in the comatose brain of Ariel Sharon, it must be the impulse to smile. After the Israeli prime minister collapsed in early 2006, his doctors tried everything they could to revive him. Familiar voices, his favourite music, even his favourites meal of sizzling meat: all failed to get a response. Perhaps they should just have whispered in his ear the words: 'You've won.'

For more than half a century, the man they called the Bulldozer had fought to prevent the creation of a Palestinian state. Then Sharon, always the master tactician, broke a great Israeli taboo by pronouncing himself in favour a Palestinian state; but, under the cover of being a convert to the cause, he succeeded in doing everything possible to delay its creation, while seizing yet more land for the Jewish state. So how had he achieved this?

Yasser Arafat, perhaps the one man who could have led his people to independence, had been discredited in the eyes of the outside world and had died in exile. The expansion of illegal Jewish settlements in East Jerusalem and the West Bank had continued apace, with only a few token words of protest from the international community. Despite the fact that the route of the infamous Wall, the structure Sharon had built deep inside the West Bank, had been ruled illegal by the International Court of Justice in The Hague, there had been no serious international pressure on Israel to end, or even limit, the expropriation of Palestinian land by making substantial adjustments to the route of the Wall.

As it nears completion, the Wall is succeeding in dividing the West Bank into cantons and separating Arab East Jerusalem from the West Bank, making it virtually impossible for a Palestinian capital to be established there. It had become a de facto border which gave Israel more than 80 percent of the total land mass between the Dead Sea and the Mediterranean.

From the beginning, the Palestinians had played into Sharon's hands. Their rejection of the reported peace offer by Sharon's predecessor, Ehud Barak, was politically valid, but they failed to explain their case properly. Instead, they resorted to violence. Unlike the first intifada, which was a popular, unarmed resistance, the second uprising was an armed conflict, led by the various militant groups. Their murderous tactic of employing suicide bombers against Jewish civilians had left the Palestinian cause almost completely bereft of meaningful foreign support.

After six years of fighting, the Palestinian national movement was in complete disarray. Fatah and Hamas were more intent on killing each other than mounting any resistance to the occupation. When a shaky administration of national unity did finally emerge, it was the worst of all worlds: a hopelessly inefficient body with no money to spend and no clear political strategy. In failing to agree on what they were trying to achieve and whether to use politics, a military campaign or a mixture of both to attain it, the Palestinian Authority perfectly mirrored the split in Palestinian society. It came as no surprise when this administration finally collapsed in the summer of 2007, leaving Palestinians with two authorities, one controlled by Fatah in the West Bank, and another controlled by Hamas in Gaza.

Since its inception, the Palestinian Authority had been ruled by a single party, the Fatah party of Yasser Arafat. When Arafat signed the Oslo Accords which created the Authority, he was giving up the struggle to liberate all of the land claimed by the Palestinians and was accepting that Palestine, when it emerged as a new country, would comprise only 22 percent of these lands. He was determined to rule over it in his own way. Chairman Arafat began calling himself 'President Arafat'. Fatah politicians, and in particular those who had served with Arafat in exile in Tunis, got all the top jobs. If you were a party man, you were looked after. Vocal opponents of the regime, by contrast, were quickly silenced. People were jailed and tortured. Despite promises to separate the judiciary from the executive power, Arafat kept a firm grip on all the levers. The international community turned a blind eye to these abuses, either because they believed that reforms were on the way or because they simply didn't care.

When Arafat died, there was no one to replace him, largely because he had spent much of the previous decade making sure that no genuinely popular leader could emerge to challenge him. And without the absolute power that Arafat had always guaranteed it, the Fatah movement struggled to maintain control over the people. When they lost the elections to Hamas in January 2006, they simply didn't know how to react. At first, Fatah leaders refused the offer, made by Hamas immediately after the election, of a unity government. When they finally agreed, it was too late. A year-long economic boycott and twelve months of mismanagement by a Hamas administration which didn't know how to govern had left the Palestinian territories in turmoil.

If Hamas needed, or pretended to need, the help of Fatah in running the political administration, they had no intention of sharing control of the military forces. Hamas wanted their own fighters and their own leaders running the armed security forces and police; Fatah, whose people dominated the various forces, were unwilling to give up that power. To make matters worse, the Americans encouraged Fatah not to give up key posts in the armed forces to Hamas, and began rearming and retraining the various units of the military. Not surprisingly, Hamas read this as a US-backed plot to mount a coup, and acted accordingly. After days of bitter fighting in which more than a hundred people were killed, Hamas fighters took control of the Palestinian security-force headquarters in the Gaza Strip.

Fatah remained too powerful in the West Bank for Hamas to challenge them, and troops loyal to President Mahmoud Abbas retained control there. Abbas dissolved the national-unity government and appointed an emergency administration. Hamas refused to accept the ruling, claiming that it was still the legitimate power in the Palestinian areas.

There are now two Palestinian authorities and two Palestinian security forces. The one in the West Bank is largely secular and backed by the Americans, the Europeans and, to some extent, the Israelis. The Gaza administration is Islamic, backed by Syria and Iran, and therefore shunned by the West. The chances of a reconciliation are slim. Negotiations aimed at establishing another administration of national unity look highly unlikely to succeed, given the bitterness between Fatah and Hamas and the fact that both the Americans and the Israelis are doing everything they can to prevent such a reconciliation from taking place.

Alternatively, Fatah could call fresh elections and let the people decide who should to run the administration. But Hamas is against any further elections, claiming that the results of the 2006 polls constitute a democratic mandate for them. Perhaps they also believe that, given the recent problems they have experienced in government, their popular support has dwindled in the interim. Those who are determined to keep Hamas out of power appear to have no strategy to achieve this other than to ignore the existence of the movement and hope that they simply fade away. In the meantime, the Palestinian territories remain deeply split, politically and militarily, and so the risk of further civil conflict remains high.

Over in Israel, they have been having their own political crisis. When Sharon slipped into a coma, the reins of power were handed to his deputy, Ehud Olmert. But Olmert had only a fragile hold on power. Sharon's earlier decision to form a new political party, Kadima, had shattered the already fragmented Israeli body politic, and no new Israeli leader can now forge a comfortable majority in Parliament to make a peace deal, even if they wished to. On his appointment as acting prime minister, Olmert had promised that Kadima would continue Sharon's policy of separation or unilateral disengagement from the Palestinian territories.

In the elections that were called in the Israeli elections of early 2006, Kadima barely held on to power, but by then the result didn't much matter because the Palestinians had elected Hamas and everything was put on hold: there were no peace talks, and no more unilateral disengagement. With Hamas refusing either to accept Israel's right to exist or to forswear violence, Israel felt that it had added justification for adopting a policy of sitting tight and doing nothing.

At the same time as it is refusing to hand back control of Palestinian land, the Israeli government is continuing to seize more of it. Not a day goes by without Israel confiscating more territory, breaking new ground, and building new homes for Jewish settlers in the West Bank. Arab communities are being squeezed into ever smaller, more remote enclaves and vital water supplies on the West Bank are being expropriated.

Despite the fact that there will soon be little land remaining on which to build a Palestinian state, the international community, and in particular the United States, has failed to act in an urgent manner. What protests the international community have made are met with Israeli assurances that it remains committed to the creation of a Palestinian state and that it is prepared to negotiate whenever the Arabs are ready to end the violence. On this point, Israel has the backing of much of the outside world – which now appears to view the conflict in the context of Palestinian violence being the cause of the continuing occupation, rather than the other way around.

A headline story in the *Jerusalem Post* newspaper in the spring of 2007 reported that the Israeli prime minister and the Palestinian president would be meeting regularly from then on. All aspects of the Palestinian state would be up for discussion, said the report, apart from 'the refugee issue, the settlements and the division of Jerusalem': in other words, none of the three main issues that are at the heart of this long war. ·

This book is an attempt to discuss these issues, and some others, with people from both communities. Are the Palestinians and the Israelis serious about creating a two-state solution? What, if anything, are they prepared to give up? And what are they willing to do in order to achieve a resolution to the conflict?

I have yet to meet a Palestinian or an Israeli who believes that this conflict will end in the next ten or even twenty years. Many think that it will never be resolved. The majority of Palestinians are convinced that Israel will not make a decent offer on statehood any time soon. Few hold out much hope that a viable, contiguous state will emerge in the near future, and believe Israel will make either a very bad offer or no offer at all. For the Arabs, this amounts to the same thing. Either way, they believe that the Israeli concept of a peace process is more about process than peace and that, in the end, it is simply a ruse to allow them to manage the conflict, while confiscating yet more Palestinian land.

On the Israeli side, the almost universal conviction is that, when they made a 'generous offer' to the Palestinians in 2000, it was rewarded by a bloody uprising. The vast majority of Israelis now accept the argument that a Palestinian state, created under the present conditions, would amount to a terrorist state. Any concessions will be seen as a sign of weakness and an encouragement for Israel to fight on in order to attain more.

Both Palestinians and Israelis now tend to see this conflict as an existential struggle: as a fight for their very survival. With little constructive contact between the two sides, there seems to be little hope of them losing this fear that they are involved in a deadly zero-sum game, in which the winner takes all and the loser gets nothing. Indeed, maybe they are right about each other: perhaps the perception has become the reality.

'The Arabs want to drive us into the sea' is a quote you hear from the Israelis time and time again. It is a reference to an Arab rallying cry from previous wars. Only a few Palestinians still use it – openly, at least. Most know that it will never happen, and say that they don't wish it to happen. Today, the majority of Palestinians say they would be content to accept a Palestinian state on the ceasefire line drawn up after the 1948 war. This would give them all of the West Bank, the Gaza Strip and the eastern half of Jerusalem – or about 22 percent of the entire land between the Jordan River and the Mediterranean Sea.

The Palestinians have been saying this for some time, but many Israelis have never accepted those assurances. In Israel, opinion polls suggest that a majority now accepts the notion of a Palestinian state, but there is a great deal of uncertainty about what is meant by this term. For instance, the opinion pollsters do not generally ask the Israeli public exactly how much land they are willing to cede control of. Even among those who support the idea of a Palestinian state, there is a huge divergence of opinion on what lands they must relinquish.

Exactly sixty years ago, the United Nations came up with a plan to partition the land then known as Palestine, which was under British control. Under the 1947 plan, the Jews were to get 55 percent of the land for a state to be called Israel; the Arabs were to get 43 percent for a Palestinian state. The 2 percent in the middle, which comprised the holy cities of Jerusalem and Bethlehem, was to be declared 'open territory' and remain under international control. After some strong-arm tactics by the United States, the members of the General Assembly narrowly voted to accept the deal.

The Jewish population of Palestine rejoiced and quickly declared the State of Israel. The mood among the Arabs was one of disappointment and anger. At the time of the vote, the Arabs made up some 65 percent of the population of the territory covered by the deal and owned more than 90 percent of the land. Not surprisingly, they rejected the agreement and began preparing for war.

The neighbouring Arab states, acting as much in their own interests as in the interests of the Palestinians, vowed to destroy the fledgling Jewish state. The Palestinians joined them in a declaration of war. The commitment of the Arab states to this war was always less than total. With the exception perhaps of Jordan, whose army had been organised by the British, the Arab troops were poorly trained and badly equipped, and there was little coordination between the various forces. The Israelis

defeated the combined Arab armies and made additional territorial gains. Instead of the generous 55 percent of the land that
had been allocated to it under the UN plan, the new Jewish
state now controlled 78 percent of the land.

Those Palestinians who were not driven off the land or fled
to the neighbouring Arab states stayed on in the remaining 22
percent, but had to live under either Jordanian or Egyptian rule.
In the Six Day War of 1967, Israel captured this remaining 22
percent, and it has maintained a military occupation of it ever
since. Arab East Jerusalem was formally annexed by the Israelis
in 1967 but has been never been recognised by the outside
world. The Palestinians were granted some limited self-autonomy through the Oslo Peace Accord of 1993, but in effect Israel
is still the ruling power in the Palestinian territories. It controls
almost every aspect of the lives of the three and a half million
Palestinians who live there.

Since the occupation began forty years ago, the Palestinian
share of the land has shrunk further. The growth of illegal
Jewish settlements in the West Bank and East Jerusalem, the
segregated roads that link these settlements, and the infamous
Wall or security barrier that now envelops these colonies has
left the Palestinians with something less than 20 percent of the
original Palestine. Most independent commentators and ana-
lysts agree that a country that is so small and so disjointed, and
has no natural resources, cannot sustain a population of that
size. The argument is that, in order for a Palestinian state to
have any chance of survival, Israel must hand back large tracts
of land – enough to create a contiguous Palestinian entity.

The Israelis say that, if the conditions are right – meaning
if their security can be guaranteed – they are prepared to talk
about handing back some territory to the Palestinians. The
unanswered question is: how much? Only fanatics and fools

believe that the Palestinians will get everything they are asking for. A few optimists think they will get what they deserve. But more and more people are coming to the conclusion that the Palestinians won't even get what they need in order to survive. Some say it's already too late. They argue that, if Israel insists on retaining most of the settlements in the West Bank, the remaining land will be too fragmented for any future Palestinian state to be sustainable.

The almost-complete absence of trust between the two sides leaves little room for negotiations on a more realistic proposal. The little good faith that existed in 2000 has been eroded by a litany of collapsed negotiations, reneged-upon deals and the vicious violence of the past seven years. The vast majority of casualties on either side have been civilians. Palestinian militants have deliberately targeted Israeli civilians, and the Israelis have used their massive firepower so indiscriminately that, despite what they say are their best efforts, more Palestinians civilians than militants have been killed.

One of the most reliable set of statistics comes from the Israeli Human Rights Organisation B'tselem, which says that, in the first six years of the current intifada, the Palestinians killed a little more than seven hundred Israeli civilians, including over a hundred children. They also killed just over three hundred members of the security forces.

B'tselem counted 1,300 Palestinian militants killed by Israeli security forces during the same period. But it also reported that 1,922 innocent Palestinian civilians had died at the hands of the Israeli security forces. Of those, more than 800 were children. Another 577 people who were killed may or may not have been involved in the fighting.

1

ONLY THE OUTSIDERS CALL IT JERUSALEM

Only the outsiders call it Jerusalem. To the Jewish population, it's 'Yerushalim'. If you're an Arab, its 'Al Quds'. For the Israelis, it's the 'permanent and indivisible' capital of the Jewish state. For the Arabs, at least half the city is the future capital of a Palestinian state. According to the UN partition plan drawn up sixty years ago, it was to be neither, but instead was to be maintained as an open city in which followers of the three great monotheistic faiths – Judaism, Islam and Christianity – could live in peace together. Over the centuries, Jerusalem has accumulated too much history and politics to be a happy place. This has helped turn a place of worship into a home for corrosive religious fervour. Heaped on top of that are all of the problems associated with a modern city, with too many people crammed into too small a space.

Driving up to Jerusalem from the coastal plain, you make a steep ascent through the wooded hills that surround the city's eastern approaches. As you round the last, gentle curve, the city begins to reveal itself. The first impression is something of a disappointment. Ugly little clusters of red-roofed apartments are huddled tightly together, as if trying to find some protection in the cracks of the pale yellow rock. As you move closer, a city becomes visible, spread out over a dozen or more undulating hills. But this is the new Jerusalem – the one built by the Israelis after 1967. The real Jerusalem, the old Jerusalem, lies concealed behind it.

As you drive towards the centre city, you notice the bright blue street signs in Hebrew, English and Arabic telling you that, just around that corner, is the Wailing Wall, or pointing you towards the ancient walls of the Old City, which have been built, destroyed and then rebuilt many times by the various invaders who laid siege here.

Ben Yehuda Street is at the heart of the new West Jerusalem. It runs down a slight incline and links a dozen or so streets in the city centre. At its summit, it is joined by King Georges Street. At its base, it broadens out into Zion Square and then fans out on to Jaffa Street and on towards the walls of the Old City.

Cobblestoned and tree-lined, Ben Yehuda is a place to pass through, or somewhere to linger. There are bookstores, street cafés and flower shops, and a dozen little food stands where people buy sizzling lamb slivers packed into pitta bread along with bundles of fresh vegetables. All along this street are the offices of the lawyers and the architects, the countless Zionist organisations, and the travel agents where weary Jerusalemites pay a couple of hundred dollars to spent three days in Turkey or Crete – or anywhere but here.

For the few foreign visitors who still come to this city, there are little shops offering antique rugs and modern jewellery, and two-thousand-year-old Dead Sea beauty products guaranteed to make you look ten years younger. The shopkeepers hang little signs in the windows that say 'big discounts for brave tourists' – a reminder to visitors of just how dangerous it is to be here, in an area which was the epicentre of the wave of suicide-bomb attacks in 2001/02.

Scores of people were killed in this part of town by the bomb attacks. Hundreds more were horribly injured. And there was immense psychological damage. The bombings become so frequent that many people began to imagine they saw suicide bombers everywhere. Real terrorism is when people became afraid of one another.

On Shlomo Hamalech Street, an Arab teenager working in a restaurant kitchen ran out for cigarettes and was almost shot as he hurried back in. An Israeli customer, a big guy sitting at an outside table and munching a bagel, pulled out a revolver and started to take aim. The owner saw it happening and literally jumped in and grabbed the weapon, just in time to stop the man pulling the trigger.

During the worst of the attacks, a lot of people were on some kind of drug. The teenagers did carry-outs of vodka and cola. The twentysomethings paid big money for cocaine, which was in increasingly short supply. Mum and Dad dug out a phone number for their old dope dealer. The grandparents got something legal from their local pharmacy.

One way or another, a large segment of Israeli society was stoned for days on end. Police reported a significant increase in the number of domestic crimes. People cooped up all day would eventually crack and start to beat each other up. Women got the worst of it. People started to drive even more erratically than usual. Fistfights broke out in the queues at the post office. The country seemed to be having a collective breakdown.

Many of the bombings were carried out by a man or a woman acting alone. But in December 2001, a team of suicide bombers hit Ben Yehuda Street with unusual and deadly efficiency. The Sabbath sunset had just brought out the thousands of young people who gathered there every Saturday night to eat ice creams and chatter about the weekend's events. The first Palestinian bomber blew himself up outside the ice-cream shop on a corner about halfway down the street. Several young people were killed. As the crowd fled screaming down the street, they ran straight into the second bomber, who immediately exploded his device, killing several more people. Within a few minutes, a third bomb went off, this time a car bomb in the next street. It had been timed to catch either fleeing survivors or rescue crews, or both. Eleven people, all under twenty years of age, died that night, and 188 more were injured and horribly maimed.

It was a devastating attack. Not just because of the death toll but because of the bombers' ability to strike at the centre of Israeli life. What really disturbed people was the manner in which the young victims had effectively been herded to their deaths. For the Jewish people, there was something particularly sinister about this. After the attacks, the streets were deserted at night. And even during the day, only those who *had* to go out were visible around Ben Yehuda.

I was staying in a little apartment just off Ben Yehuda Street around that time. Friday afternoons and Saturday mornings, when Muslims and Jews were at prayer, were the only times you could be reasonably sure there would be no attacks. But on Saturday nights and Sunday mornings, the fear was unavoidable. Like many of the people working and living in the city centre, I experienced that sense that the person beside me was a suicide bomber. Sometimes the feeling lasted for only a few seconds; other times it lasted longer. The first time it happened, I was walking to the newsagent's when I saw a man walking towards me who fitted the 'terrorist' profile perfectly, even down to his smile. (As the bombings became more frequent, people had learned that the blast from the explosives belt will sometimes lift the bomber's head clean off his body and toss it intact five or ten metres from the blast site. Several eye witnesses who had seen this reported that, to their horror, the bomber had a smile on his face. This was the chilling smile of a man who believed that he was on his way to paradise and an encounter with seventy-two virgins.)

When I saw the young Arab walking towards me, wearing a bulky overcoat and a strange smile, the notion took hold that he was a suicide bomber on a mission. A part of your brain tells you that this cannot be true, and you fight the urge to turn and run. I remember thinking that, if I turned and ran then, I might as well keep going until I reached the airport. So I looked him straight in the eyes and smiled back. I don't know why, but I had an idea that this might deter him. At worst, he was not going to have the momentary satisfaction of terrorising me. But the man passed me and didn't explode. I stood watching him for a few minutes before deciding that he was just an Arab teenager wandering through West Jerusalem. I also wondered whether he was having a little bit of sick fun that morning.

The terror from the real suicide bombers reached its peak during the current intifada, but the deadly campaign actually began several years before that. During the peace talks, the tactic was developed by Hamas and used, successfully, to derail the negotiations. The Elhannon family was among the first victims.

The Elhannons are third-generation Jerusalemites. Both sides of the family lost relatives in the Holocaust. One of the grandfathers, Motti Peled, was a hero of the war of 1948. He had

27

helped draw up the state's declaration of independence, and went on to become a member of the Israeli parliament. Motti's grandson Elik Elhannon had served with the Israeli army too. Ten years ago, when he was away on a special mission in Lebanon, Palestinian suicide bombers killed Elik's little sister on Ben Yehuda Street.

Smadar Elhannon was a beautiful, smart girl of fourteen. Elik and his brothers gave her a hard time about liking school and enjoying doing her homework. But it was just friendly teasing, and the lads really admired their little sister's ambition. Smadar wanted to be a doctor or a dancer. Or maybe both.

Like many Israeli families, the Elhannons talked a lot of politics. They had tired of the endless wars and wanted to live in peace with their Palestinian neighbours. Smadar had caught the bug early. When she was just ten, she had a letter published in one of the national newspapers calling on Israeli leaders to do more to make peace with the Palestinians.

On the morning of her death, Smadar told her mother that she and her best friend, Sivane, were going into Jerusalem for an audition at a dancing school. She said that, before the audition, they were going to the city centre to buy some school books. Her mother, Nurit, felt that it wasn't safe, and offered to drive the teenagers to a shopping centre on the outskirts of the city. Smadar was having none of it: she wanted to go, and that was it. Tired of the argument, Nurit gave in and told her to be careful.

That afternoon, three Palestinian suicide bombers from the West Bank city of Nablus arrived in Jerusalem and blew themselves up in the area where the teenagers were shopping. Smadar's father, Rami, was driving in his car when the radio news announced the attack. Reports said that five people were dead and hundreds were injured. Rami got a call from his wife to say that a family friend had reported seeing Smadar in the street where the attack happened a short time before the explosion.

Rami drove home and picked up Nurit, and together they began the awful trail around the hospitals looking for their daughter. Whey they couldn't locate her, they hoped that this meant that she was alive and drinking coffee with her friends elsewhere. Eventually they returned to the shopping centre, where someone had drawn up a list of the people who had died. The name of Smadar Elhannon was on the list.

The Elhannons are not unusual. Hundreds of Israeli families have lost loved ones in these attacks, which are completely random. The family had always been left-wing: even when there had not been much support for the idea in Israel, they had been strongly in favour of granting the Palestinians independence. The murder of their daughter made it very difficult for them to hold on to that view.

'I could have gone either way after they murdered my little sister,' Illik told me. 'It is very, very easy to be swept along by the strong emotions when you live in a tight-knit community. This is especially true if you are in the army. There, people will tell you that this happened because the Arabs are all murderers, and we have to get them back, and stuff like that. It is difficult to stop and think.'

But Elik *did* stop and think, and so did his parents. When some Israeli politicians began to use Smadar's death to call for retaliation, the family spoke out publicly against such a move, and told the politicians to stop using her family's loss to promote their own political agenda. Some Israelis understood what they were trying to say, but many did not, and the Elhannons were denounced in some quarters as traitors and 'self-hating Jews'.

Elik denies that he is some kind of peacenik. 'I have no willingness to forgive,' he says. 'I am not forgiving anyone. The person who kills a child has committed a heinous crime, and there is no excuse. But the thing to do is not to hate as a result and not to seek revenge.'

Elik Elhannon is now one of the leading members of an organisation called Combatants for Peace. At least that's what the former Israeli soldiers in the group call it. The Palestinian membership, mainly drawn from the mainstream Al Aqsa Martyrs Brigade, call it Fighters for Peace. The organisation is made up of Palestinians and Israelis who have given up the gun and try to promote understanding through cross-community dialogue. It all sounds a bit worthy and maybe even somewhay pointless. But you can't help but admire their efforts. I met Elik in Tel Aviv, where he is studying literature at one of the city's two universities. For Elik, the most important part of the course is his study of various writings in Hebrew. He loves his culture and his country. He just dislikes what his country is doing. And what the army in which he served is doing.

Before forming Combatants for Peace, Elik Elhannon was part of a conscientious-objector movement called Courage to Refuse. 'That started with a big bang,' he says. 'Someone predicted that if we had 500 members, the earth would shake. Well, we had 635 members, and the earth did not shake.' Elik was one of those who felt that the movement was not going anywhere. 'This was why the idea of a new group involving Palestinian militants was so compelling,' he remembers.

Even finding a meeting place for the new group is difficult. The Palestinians cannot come into Jerusalem; the Israelis are not allowed to enter the West Bank. They gather, at night, in seedy little hotels and cafés along the border, the sort of places which are used by people who have something to hide. Among the spies, the criminals and the people having affairs, Arabs and Israelis meet to discuss how to end the violence. At the meetings, each person tells what he did, and why he did it. And, most importantly, what made him stop. 'We say that, if we can talk and we can co-operate after what we did and what happened, then anyone can,' Elik explains.

Elik believes that the problem is not the radicals on both sides, but the fact that 'the vast majority on either side says nothing and does nothing'. The aim of the group is to reach out to the silent majorities to 'show them there is something they can do'.

They are not a conscientious-objector movement, but one of their first rules is an adherence to non-violence. You cannot be a member of the group if you are still involved in the fighting. The Palestinians simply leave the paramilitary group they were in. Mostly this happens after they get out of prison. For the Israelis, who can be called up every year for army reserve duty, things are different. 'Exactly how to avoid serving is up to them,' says Elik. 'If you refuse [to serve], and go to prison, that's one way. If you sign a piece of paper saying you're crazy, that's another. Or maybe you can cut a deal with your commander so you will do your reserve duty only in Israel.'

Many Israelis consider Elik and his group to be disloyal or even treasonous. He knows that he is probably being watched by the secret police. 'We think that refusing to support the military occupation is the truly patriotic thing to do,' he says. 'We are not bleeding hearts, and we are certainly not enemies of Israel.'

Combatants for Peace organises regular public meetings in Israel and in the Palestinian territories. They encourage the public to listen by first recounting their own experiences. 'We don't bore people with facts,' says Elik. 'We don't apologise. We are not asking for forgiveness from anyone but simply presenting our personal position. We don't always convince people. But we manage to get respect, and once we get respect we can start to engage in dialogue.'

While the former Israeli soldiers risk hostility at home, surely they risk death when they cross into the Palestinian territories? 'I don't know if it is dangerous,' says Elik. 'I know that it is always frightening. But for the past six years, not one peace activist from Israel has been hurt in Palestine. Whether this is sheer luck or Palestinian will, I do not know. When I was in the army, I was putting myself in danger. What I am doing now is not more dangerous.'

The concern over whether the members of the group are genuine about peace is a concern for both sides, reinforced each time new people join. They could be spies or assassins. 'We don't know for sure,' says Elik. 'But we believe. That's where the faith comes in. We trust them. And they trust us.'

While the former fighters are talking, the politicians are not. Right now, no Israeli leader will dare talk to Hamas. This is a political imperative: their rivals would use the information to destroy them. But, according to Elik, the idea of talking to Hamas takes the discussion into what he calls the realm of 'the Israeli psychosis'.

'We are very much afraid of Hamas. But what can Hamas do? They don't have tanks, they don't have nuclear weapons, and they don't have chemical weapons. What can they do? They can blow up some buses. But this, by definition, is just terrorism. They cannot destroy the State of Israel. So why are we so afraid of them?'

The complication now is that there are other players involved: Iran on the side of Hamas and America on the side of Israel. According to Elik, Israelis and Palestinians each run the risk of losing control of the situation. But he believes that what successive Israeli governments really fear is not the failure of talks with Hamas but the possibility of the success of such talks. If a peace process begins, then the Jewish state will have to make real compromises.

'This is the only explanation,' he says. 'This government is not representative of the people's wishes. The people repeatedly say that they want a two-state solution based roughly on the lines of the 1967 ceasefire. Yet this government's policies seem to work counter to that.' Elik spends a lot of time with his group of former army comrades visiting high schools in Israel and talking to teenagers of about seventeen or eighteen years of age. 'I frequently meet people who do not know what the occupation means,' he says. 'They don't even know what lands we occupy.'

Combatants for Peace believe that the organisation faces two challenges. They want to confront those Israelis who believe that peace is not possible, and they have to reinforce the beliefs of those who believe that it is. 'We want to put a crack in the wall of indifference,' says Elik.

According to Elik, many ordinary Israelis are so despairing of the situation that they are leaving Israel. 'Something like a million Israeli citizens now live abroad,' he says. 'In all, some 750,000 people have gone to America. It's not just about the work and the money: there is something seriously wrong back here.'

Elik Elhannon reminds me that he comes from a very Zionist family. 'It hurts me that this project is dying and that it's the occupation that is bringing that about,' he says. Elik doesn't see much sign of a real peace deal on the way. 'Nothing in the short term,' he says, but adds that there are 'major changes taking place on both sides', including alliances which were unthinkable before now. 'This is the right time to propose something new,' he asserts. What that something might be is a question he cannot answer.

*

'Give us two billion dollars a year for weapons, and we promise not to use the suicide operations,' says Ibrahim, a twenty-two-year-old student at Beir Zeit University, just outside Ramallah. After talking to Elik, I have come to the university to talk to some young Palestinians about whether they support the campaign of violence. After much persuading, a group agree to talk to me. They are highly suspicious of the media. They say they are not members of the militant groups but that they do support them. The ones who agree to talk will not tell me their surnames. They say that they could be identified by the Israeli intelligence services and hauled in and interrogated.

'We do not want to kill ourselves,' says Ibrahim, when I ask him about the suicide bombings. 'The Jewish already kill too many of us,' he continues, 'and we don't want to kill Israeli babies, so give us the money and we will fight the Israelis like a real army.'

During the worst of the fighting, many Palestinians either supported the suicide bombers or were ambivalent about the tactic. Until recently, few people would come out and condemn them. Opinion polls suggested that around 50 percent were in favour of suicide attacks, but that figure tended to rise after an Israeli air raid or incursion in which people died. Most people would try to explain their support for suicide attacks by claiming that it was not about the killing of Israelis simply because they were Israelis. It was, they explained, about 'parity of pain'. The rationale was that they had to let the Israelis know that there was a high price to be paid for the occupation, and the killing of Palestinians.

The real question for these students is whether they would be willing to be a suicide bomber themselves. There is silence when I ask this question. They look at each other and say nothing. I wait, then repeat the question, this time directing it at Ibrahim.

'No, I don't want to be a bomber,' he says. 'It is not for me. But I support any man who makes the martyrdom operation. He is a good Palestinian. He fights for his people.'

friend Mahmoud shuts him up. 'Always on the TV, t the suicide bombers, always the suicide bombers.

Never you [sic] ask about the Palestinian women and children the Israeli kill.'

Then one of the young women speaks up. 'You call us terrorists,' she says, 'but why are we the terrorists?' She tells me her name is Rheema and that she is nineteen. She has her head covered and is wearing a long grey dress. 'You say the occupation is wrong but you say also it is wrong to fight the Israelis. What do you want us to do, lie down and die?'

I tell her people say that they are terrorists only if they kill innocent civilians. 'This is not the truth,' she says. 'You say Palestinians are terrorists if they kill Israeli soldiers also. Why is this terrorism if the Israeli soldiers put us under occupation? When the Israelis kill our children, is this not terrorism? Why you don't [sic] call the Israelis terrorists? They kill us so that they can take our land but you don't say this. If we do not fight, how will the world know that the Palestinian people are under occupation?'

What about politics? I ask. Is there not a political way of dealing with this problem? 'The Palestinian people have tried politics,' answers Mahmoud, 'and it has not worked because the Israelis do not care for peace. When we said to them that we will accept a Palestinian state on a small piece of our land and let us use politics to make peace, they say OK, and then they build the wall and take more land. They think we are weak, and so they take what they want.'

Another young man, who introduces himself as Salah, speaks for the first time. 'We are weak,' he says. 'We are weak because we have no friends. Even our brothers in the other Arab countries do not help us. They will do nothing. The only time people see what is going on here is when bad things happen. Then everybody says they must do something. There is talking and talking but nobody will do anything to help us. So we fight.'

I ask what they learned in school about the Israelis and

about the Jewish nation. Were they being taught to hate the Jews? 'This is what the Israelis are saying,' responds Rheema. 'But this is not true. The schools teach us that the Jewish people take our land. This is the truth. We know this is the truth because we see this happen now. It does not mean that we hate all the Israelis. We have to live with them. We know this, but maybe they do not know that we live here too.'

2

FROM ONE-HORSE TOWN TO DEAD-END TOWN

Even before 1967, the West Bank village of Anata was a one-horse town. But after the Six Day War, the Israelis cut it in half and turned it into a dead-end town. When the Israelis captured the West Bank and subsequently annexed a vast tract of land around the east side of Jerusalem, a section of Anata became part of the newly expanded municipality of the city. The annexation was illegal, and is recognised by no one except Israel; nonetheless Anata is divided and has been cut off from its natural hinterland.

Before 1967, Anata was connected to a number of neighbouring villages: Hizma to the north, Shu'fat to the west, and Al Issawiya to the south. Most of the residents of Anata made their living from its seven or eight thousand acres of agricultural land. After part of the village and much of the surrounding land was incorporated into the expanded municipal boundaries of Jerusalem, many people lost their source of income and were forced to leave the villages forever.

When half of Anata was annexed, the Israelis assumed control over half of the villagers too. In East Jerusalem and in scores of small Arab communities close to Jerusalem, tens of thousands of Palestinians whose lands and homes were captured and then annexed were given a choice: they could either become 'citizens' of Israel or could be classed as 'permanent residents' of Israel. Either way, they were losing part of their Palestinian identity. The majority opted for the blue ID card which represented 'permanent residency' status. Permanent residents have far fewer rights than citizens. Essentially, they are like permanent visitors to Israel, even though they didn't go to Israel, Israel came to them.

Today, about a third of Anata's population of some twelve thousand people hold blue identity cards. The other two-thirds, who live in the part of the town that has not been annexed but is under military occupation, are classified as West Bank residents. West Bank residents cannot enter Jerusalem without a special pass – which is very hard to get. For Anata, this means that the people from the western part of the village cannot get into the eastern part. The infamous West Bank Wall, which now cuts right through the township, literally cements that separation.

The misery doesn't end there. The amount of land expropriated by Israel prevents any possible expansion of the village. According to the Israeli human-rights organisation the Committee Against House Demolitions, the Israeli authorities expropriated some five thousand acres of land from Anata in order to build the West Bank settlements of Alon, Kfar Adumim, Almon and Ma'aleh Adumim. These settlements, together with their service roads and the Anatot military base, completely surround the village, leaving it isolated from its remaining agricultural lands.

Forty-two-year-old Bassam Aramin lives in the West Bank half of Anata with his wife Shulwa and their five children. When he was a teenager, Bassam spent seven years in an Israeli jail for the attempted killing of a number of IDF (Israeli Defence Forces) soldiers. After getting out of jail, Bassam quit the armed resistance. For years, he concentrated on his work and on raising his family. But when the cross-community peace group Combatants for Peace was formed, Bassam joined up immediately, and he quickly emerged as one of its most effective spokesmen. He had something to say, and he could say it in fluent Hebrew, having picked up the language during his years spent in prison.

Each week, Bassam joined the small group of Palestinians and Israelis who were touring the halls and meetings rooms around Israel and the Palestinian territories, telling their stories and promoting non-violence. His enthusiasm for the project soon rubbed off on some of his family, particularly his ten-year-old daughter Abir. She tried many times to get her father to take her to the public meetings he was attending. He said no, but helped her join one of the summer camps funded by foreign governments, at which groups of Arab and Israeli children would meet and get to know a little about each other. After several meetings, Abir had even begun to learn a few words of Hebrew so that she could talk to her new Israeli friends. Then she was shot dead.

Bassam had grown up in Hebron, a city to the south of Jerusalem. When he was still in his teens, he took part in a demonstration against the occupation. At the time, Palestinian national emblems were deemed illegal by the occupying forces and Bassam was beaten up by a couple of Israeli soldiers simply for waving the Palestinian flag. From there, it was a quick journey to more serious action for him. He and a couple of other teenagers got their hands on a number of old rifles and a couple of hand grenades and tried to attack an Israeli patrol. The operation failed miserably and Bassam was caught and sentenced to seven years in jail.

Bassam says that, in prison, he was beaten and humiliated on a regular basis. Then one night, the prison authorities showed a film about the Holocaust. Bassam watched it with interest and for the first time understood something about the Israelis' position. That realisation helped open up some communication with several of the prison guards. One night, one of them asked Bassam why the Palestinians hated the Israelis so much. For Bassam, this was something of a revelation: he could not fathom how any Israeli could not understand why the Palestinians were fighting them. As he began to tell his story to the prison guard, Bassam realised that the Israeli knew nothing of what life under occupation was like. And the guard appeared to know still less about how the arrival in Palestine of hundreds of thousands of Jews after the Second World War had destroyed the lives of the Palestinians who had been living there.

When Bassam was freed from jail, he managed to stay out of trouble. He got married and got a job as a researcher with the Palestinian National Archive. When he heard about Fighters for Peace being formed, he remembered the prison guard and thought that it might be a good idea to use his experiences to tell other Israelis what was really going on in the Palestinian areas. He wanted to tell them why the Palestinians were fighting, and how they didn't hate all Jews.

In community halls and college campus buildings throughout Israel, Bassam stood in front of small gatherings of the sceptical, the curious and even the downright hostile, and told them: 'I am the terrorist you fear, now deal with me.' From the reponses he got, he felt that he was getting somewhere.

One morning early in 2007, Bassam was getting ready to go

to work in Ramallah. It was just a short drive from his village of Anata, so he had time to play and chat with his children as they got ready for school. Abir, his nine-year-old daughter, told him that, when she finished her exams later that morning, she was going to a friend's house to study, and would be late home. 'No you're not,' he told her firmly. 'You'll come straight back here and I'll help you study when I get home from work.'

A few hours later, he got the phone call. His daughter had been shot by Israeli security forces outside the school. Friends had taken her to the hospital in Ramallah, but her head wounds were so serious that she needed emergency surgery, and Ramallah didn't have the facilities to carry out the surgery effectively. Bassam used his connections with the peace group to obtain permission to take Abir to the well-equipped Israeli hospital in West Jerusalem. The surgeons there tried their best to save Abir, but her injuries were too severe. Abir died a couple of days later.

The killing was bad enough, but what happened afterwards compounded the pain for the family. First, the Israelis suggested that his little girl had been hit by a stone thrown by a Palestinian youth who was attacking a police patrol. A number of stones had been thrown by some other kids that morning but, given the extent of the little girl's head injuries, this explanation was clearly ludicrous.

There followed a report on Israeli television quoting unnamed security sources as saying that Abir had been playing with some kind of explosive device and that it had gone off in her hand. This suggestion made Bassam very angry. 'Her fingers were whole and her head had exploded? They are liars,' he said at the time.

His twelve-year-old daughter Arin, who had been with Abir at the time, told how the two little girls had been running away

41

from the stone-throwing incident when the police began to fire rubber bullets. Abir was hit, and fell. After the shooting stopped, Arin picked up a rubber bullet from the roadside where her little sister had been shot. The autopsy carried out by the Israelis revealed that the little girl had been hit in the back of the head by a hard object, but the report stopped short of saying that it had been a rubber bullet.

A full inquiry has been ordered, but Bassam does not expect any useful result from it. He thinks that the border policeman responsible for his daughter's death will either be acquitted or be given a lenient sentence. Bassam is still waiting for the outcome of the inquiry.

Despite all that has happened, Bassam Aramin is determined to carry on working with the peace group. 'I'm not going to exploit the blood of my child for political purposes,' he told the newspaper *Ha'aretz*. 'I am not going to lose my common sense and my direction because I have lost my heart, my child. I will continue to fight to protect her brothers and sisters, her friends, both Palestinian and Israeli. They are all our children.'

On the Fighters for Peace website, Bassam wrote: 'It would be easy, so easy, to hate. To seek revenge, find my own rifle, and kill three or four soldiers, in my daughter's name. That's the way Israelis and Palestinians have run things for a long time. Every dead child – and everyone is someone's child – is another reason to keep killing. But the only way to make it stop is to stop it ourselves.'

I went to see Bassam at the Palestinian National Archive on the outskirts of Ramallah. With one other worker, he shares a small office piled high with newspapers waiting to be indexed. A small gas stove gives off an orange glow but very little heat. Bassam is wearing a short tweed coat and a *keffiyeh* (the Palestinian scarf). He speaks softly. His English is good, but he pauses sometimes, as if to remember the words and ideas he has spoken and written many times.

I ask him about the peace group and about how difficult is must be for him to maintain cordial relations with former Israeli soldiers after what has happened to his family. He tells me that several Israeli members of the group stayed with him after his daughter was shot. They were at the hospital; they were at his home. 'I have come to love them like brothers,' he says. 'These are men who have come to know my past. They are men who, like me, were trained to hate and to kill, but who now believe that we must find a way to live with our former enemies.'

Many Palestinians simply won't get involved in any peace group which has Israeli members because it can never be a partnership of equals. The Palestinians are the ones under occupation; the Israelis are the occupiers. How does that Bassam answer that one? 'It is true, we are not equal. It is very easy to fight and very easy to resist, and it is very difficult to sit down and talk with the ones who are occupying your lands and killing your people, but we have to do it.'

Has he met with any strong objections from friends or neighbours to his involvement with the group since his daughter's killing? 'Nobody told me to stop. They respect me,' he says. 'Besides, I would not stop. I believe what I do. It makes me stronger in my resolve to continue.'

Bassam says that the Palestinians do not have any choice but to continue the group's peace efforts. We must put an end to the occupation, and if someone from the Israeli side agrees with that, they will be our friend. Actually, we are fighting for peace and not for the Palestinians or the Israelis.'

I ask him how much he understands of why the Israelis are doing what they are doing. 'The Jewish people are afraid of another Holocaust,' he says. 'But the Palestinian people are paying a terrible price for that fear. We are the victims of the victim. We should not be paying because of their fears and their suffering.'

When Bassam attends public meetings in Israel, he speaks for a few minutes first and then takes part in a question-and-answer session. 'I ask the Israelis how they can have full diplomatic relations with the Germans, the ones who caused all their suffering, yet they will not allow us to have our own state. And I ask them how they can do such things to us when they have suffered so much at the hands of the Nazis and others.'

He says that the usual Israeli reply to such questions is that the Holocaust and Israel's treatment of Palestinians are not the same. What is his answer to that? 'I say to them: you are right, they are not the same. I tell them that what they are doing is worse, because they must really know this feeling of bitterness. They must remember what it is like to suffer, and yet they make us suffer.'

For Bassam, the important task is to try to make the Israelis understand Palestinian suffering, because only the Israelis can end it, 'not the Palestinians, not the Americans or the Europeans, and not the Iranians. It is only the Israelis who can do it,' he says, 'and they *have* to do it, because they are suffering too.'

I put it to him that most Israelis are a long way from that conclusion and that, right now, many of them view the Palestinians only as an enemy. Their aim is not to help them but to defeat them. Bassam believes that this attitude is bred into Israelis very early in their life, and particularly when they do their national service, usually at the age of eighteen. 'When they are in the army, they look at us as the targets,' he says. 'Some of the soldiers we now deal with served for five years, and they never saw a Palestinian as anything other than a terrorist. They saw us at checkpoints every day. They searched us. They beat us. They tortured us. They shot us. They never saw us as people.'

'They send their kids to the army at eighteen or nineteen, and they are just children. What do they know? When you are eighteen and you are given an M16 [rifle] and told that the Palestinians are your enemy and that if you shoot them you will have no responsibility for your actions, that you will never go to jail or even to trial, then that is what you will do, and that is what many of them do.'

I ask Bassam about the prospects for peace. I put it to him that, despite six years of bitter fighting, the opinion polls in Israel suggest that there is still a majority in favour of the establishment of a Palestinian state.

He is sceptical about the real feelings of Israelis. 'Right now, only a small number of Israelis want real peace – that is, peace with justice,' he argues. 'Many of the Israelis just want peace, but they also want to maintain the occupation. They want peace, but they want to keep the settlements, and they want to keep the refugees out, and they want to keep all of Jerusalem. Many of them are racist, racist in their blood. They want an apartheid regime like what [the whites] had in South Africa.'

At the same time, he firmly believes that things will get better, because the present situation cannot continue. 'How much longer can this go on?' he asks. 'Can they really occupy us for another forty years? We cannot accept that, and the Israelis should not accept that.'

In one of his meetings with the Israelis, a former soldier put it to him that he couldn't go for a cup of coffee in Tel Aviv without worrying about being blown up. Bassam's response was that the Israelis would continue to walk in danger until a Palestinian could drink coffee in Hebron without being afraid. 'If you agree to be part of what makes another people suffer, then you must suffer also,' he told his Israeli counterpart.

For Bassam, the decision to end military resistance is as much about its lack of effectiveness as it is about anything else. 'To fight is our right,' he says. 'We must be able to resist. But we cannot defeat Israel by force. There is no comparison between these military forces: we are not the same. We do not have any choice but to talk.'

I ask him why he feels that the Israelis should talk to the Palestinians after all that has happened. 'The Israelis have bad memories of what was done to them in the Holocaust. Well, we have long memories too, and we will not let them forget what they are doing to us now. Therefore they must talk too.'

Before I leave, I ask Bassam how his wife Shalwa and his five young children are coping with the loss of Abir. 'It is very difficult for my wife,' he says. 'The day is very hard, but she gets through it. The night is another life. For now, I cannot explain to the other children what happened.'

Then he tells me that Arin, the twelve-year-old who was with Abir when she was killed, was asked by a journalist how her father could continue working with the Israelis. The little girl had replied: 'I trust my father, but if the Israelis continue to kill Palestinians, I will advise him to go away from them and stop talking to them.'

*

The Israeli government repeatedly points out that, with very few exceptions, the deaths of Palestinian civilians at the hands of security forces are accidental. Their spokespeople are at pains to contrast this with the deaths of Israeli civilians who have been deliberately targeted by the Palestinian militants.

Israel claims that, despite the fact that it is fighting against terrorist organisations which ignore the rules of war, their security forces continue to act with restraint. And it resents any suggestion to the contrary. According to Yossi Klein Halevi, the Israel correspondent for *New Republic* magazine, 'The relentless criticism of our conduct of this war is experienced as a kind of psychological terrorism, a second front in the war against our being.'

Writing in a pamphlet published by the American Jewish Committee, Halevi argues that 'Many Israelis, including political moderates, believe that Israel has repeatedly erred on the side of restraint'. He says that 'Accusations of excessive force are greeted by Israelis with dismay or bitter cynicism'. He goes on to quote figures for the numbers dead as of January 2005, comparing the number of Israelis killed with the number of Palestinians who have died. The finding he draws from this comparison is that three-quarters of the Israelis who have been killed were innocent civilians, while fewer than half of the Palestinians could be classed as non-combatants. In other words, that Israel behaves in a far more humane manner than its enemies.

But this ignores the total number of people killed on each side, and the disparity between the two. And these figures reveal a different picture. When it comes to the killing of innocent civilians, the Israeli Defence Forces have killed well over twice as many, by accident, as the Palestinian militants have killed deliberately. Put more starkly, as many as 1,922 Palestinian men, women and children, all innocent civilians, have been killed 'unintentionally' by the Israeli security forces.

The Israeli Defence Forces spokespeople frequently refer to the force as 'the Most Moral Army in the World'. But what is moral about an army that kills as many innocent civilians as it does terrorists? If the IDF is not acting in an immoral manner, then it must be hopelessly incompetent. But they get away with this level of killing because very few cases of wrongful deaths are properly investigated, and in the ones that are, the culprits generally receive very lenient sentences.

Let me give you a recent example. A couple of years ago, a thirteen-year-old Palestinian schoolgirl was shot dead near a checkpoint in Gaza. Iman Al Hamas was walking home, dressed in a school uniform and carrying her schoolbag on her back. When she approached an Israeli army checkpoint, the soldiers shouted at her to stop and turn back. Whether she did not hear the command or just ignored it is not known. In any event, she kept walking. The soldiers opened fire, and the little girl was hit and fell to the ground.

One of the officers at the checkpoint then left his post and walked over to where the little girl was lying. To the horror of some of his comrades, he fired a number of shots from his automatic weapon into the body of the child. When he was asked by fellow soldiers what he had been doing, he told them that he was 'just confirming the kill'.

The incident, which came to light only when some of the officer's colleagues 'swore out' a formal complaint against him, caused widespread outrage in Israel as well as in the Palestinian territories. The army promised a full investigation. The result of that investigation was reported by *Ha'aretz* newspaper in the spring of 2007. The paper told how the soldier, an officer serving with the Givati Brigade, was due to receive 80,000 shekels (about €12,000) in compensation from the state after he was cleared of all charges in relation to the death of Iman Al Hamas.

According to the report, Captain 'R' will receive compensation from the state in addition to a reimbursement of several hundred euro in legal expenses, as part of an arrangement which was reached between his lawyers and the military prosecution. The *Ha'aretz* report continued that 'the officer, who at the time of the incident was serving as a company commander, has since been promoted to major, and is currently serving as an operations officer'.

The judges who acquitted Captain R accepted his version of events, in which he stated that the shots that he had fired were not aimed directly at the girl's body. Captain R told the court that he had opened fire in order to create a 'deterrence', and that he believed that the young girl posed 'a serious threat' to himself and his comrades. The judges also criticised the Military Police's investigation of the case, which was based upon a poor transcription of recorded evidence and upon the testimonies of disgruntled soldiers serving under Captain R – the implication being that they made up part or all of their testimony.

Gideon Levy is an Israeli journalist who investigates possible wrongful killings by the IDF. Each week, in the Friday edition of *Ha'aretz*, in a feature entitled 'Twilight Zone', Levy reports on the latest Palestinian civilians to have been killed by the Israeli security forces. Some of the cases appear to be genuine accidents, such as inevitably occur in the heat of battle, but others appear to be cases of callous disregard for human life, and still others are clearly the result of indiscriminate shooting. Some cases look very like murder – or at least enough like murder to merit a full investigation.

With more than 1,900 civilian deaths so far in the current intifada, there is no shortage of work for Levy. Even if the violence were to stop completely tomorrow, he would have enough cases to keep him busy for at least another ten years, and maybe twenty, he says.

His investigations, in which he talks in detail to eye witnesses and the victim's families, are one of the few attempts at independent inquiry into the deaths of Palestinian civilians. In the vast majority of the cases, the army investigates itself. Levy tells me that he cannot remember how many of the cases have been fully investigated, and proper findings published. He says that maybe a handful of killings have resulted in disciplinary action against the soldiers involved.

When Levy contacts the defence forces for a comment, they usually simply reply that they are investigating the case. 'I judge them from the results,' he says. 'Usually there are no investigations, and even when there are probes, I don't hear from them any more. They don't appear to be dealing with these cases in a serious manner.'

Levy is a former political advisor to former Israeli prime minister and Nobel Peace Prize winner Shimon Peres, who is now president of Israel. Levy gave up politics to try to alert Israeli society to the human-rights abuses caused by the occupation. When he talks about what is happening, he appears more depressed than angry at the scale of the abuse. He says that no one seems to be taking any notice of the crimes that are being committed, and on which he is regularly reporting.

Levy believes that there is no political or public pressure on the Israeli defence forces to be fully accountable. 'Israelis are tending not to take responsibility for what is happening and to pretend not to know about what is unpleasant. This is moral blindness,' he says.

Levy's concerns are not just for the innocent Palestinians or in relation to the impact of the violence on wider Arab society. 'The damage to Israeli society will be much deeper than the damage being done to the Palestinians,' he asserts. 'The younger generation of Israelis is growing up with no idea of what is legal and what is not, or what is moral and what is immoral.' According to Levy, there is not even a debate about what is happening. 'It's a non-issue,' he tells me. 'It is not discussed. There is no information, and there is certainly no real debate about how the occupation is enforced.'

For his efforts to raise these topics, Levy receives a large amount of hate mail, and even death threats. He gets some compliments too. But why does he do it? 'Because nobody else is doing it,' he replies.

And what of the Palestinians? How are they reacting to the killings and to the virtual silence from Israeli society about what is happening? 'They will believe that there is no justice,' he says. 'They will see that justice does not come with a military occupation, and that it is ridiculous to expect it to.'

3

THE SUICIDE BOMBER

Two years ago Mohammad, or 'Hamad' for short, agreed to carry out a suicide bombing inside Israel. The only reason he and maybe a dozen or so innocent Israeli civilians are alive is because the operation was cancelled at the last minute. Hamad had already recited his final prayers. Before he could strap on the bomb belt, the news came through that the Israeli troops were waiting for him.

'We think it was an informer,' he told me through an interpreter. 'There were checkpoints all around the city. Our leadership decided to wait until another time.' Then came the ceasefire. Hamad the Martyr was laid off. 'I am an unemployed *shaheed* [martyr],' he tells me with a laugh. Hamad is wearing a ski-mask through which only his eyes can be seen. From his voice, I guess that he is probably in his late teens or early twenties.

When I met Hamad, in the spring of 2007, the suicide bombings had been temporarily suspended by all the militant groups, bar Islamic Jihad. Hamad is a member of the Al Aqsa Martyrs Brigade, which has close links with the Fatah Party headed by Palestinian president Mahmoud Abbas. Since he became president, Abbas has been quietly working to convince the militant groups to end the suicide-bombing attacks. Abbas argued that the campaign was harming the Palestinian cause. The fact that he framed his argument in those terms and would not condemn the attacks as immoral or illegal was taken as proof by many Israelis that Abbas was a 'pragmatist' rather than a 'peacemaker', and to be viewed with suspicion..

Whatever Abbas felt about the morality of the attacks, he could not state these views publicly without alienating what little popular support he had at the time. But the militant groups respect Abbas, and eventually he succeeded. The groups framed their ending of the suicide-bombing campaign in the context of an overall ceasefire, which avoided confronting the specific issue of suicide bombings. And it left the door open to using the tactic again, should the ceasefires collapse and the violence begin again in earnest.

But why did the Palestinians resort to suicide bombings in the first place? In particular, why did they continue with them when they provoked such harsh military reprisals from the IDF and gave Prime Minister Ariel Sharon a perfect pretext to attack Palestinian cities and practically destroy the Palestinian Authority. Moreover, the suicide bombings helped rally public support in Israel for the deadly incursions into the West Bank and Gaza Strip, and they silenced anyone in the international community who was inclined to speak out in support of the Palestinians.

American acquiescence to Israeli military operations, like the massive 'Defensive Shield' invasion of the West Bank in 2002, came about largely because of the revulsion at the suicide bombers. The United States was still reeling from the 9/11 attacks when the Palestinians began to step up their campaign. It was as if the Palestinian leadership saw the horrific images of the destruction of the Twin Towers as an encouragement rather than a reason to end the suicide attacks. By the time they stopped the campaign, three years later, they had lost a great deal of sympathy for the cause of Palestinian nationalism.

At the time of writing, the suicide bombings have been suspended. But among many of the militants, there remains the belief that suicide bombings are not only justifiable, but a necessary element of their armed strategy. This is not just a conviction born out of religious fervour or fundamentalism; it is an idea that still holds sway among the secular armed groups, like the Al Aqsa Martyrs Brigade, and also the PFLP (the Popular Front for the Liberation of Palestine), which leans more to communism than Islam.

Hamad is convinced that he is on an Israeli death list, but he says he cannot be sure of this. The informer may only have told the Israelis that a bombing operation was being planned, but he could have given them Hamad's name, so Hamad is not taking any chances. He could be arrested at any time, but it's more likely that the Israelis will just kill him, whether with a single shot by a sniper or in an air strike. I insist on meeting him in a refugee camp, in the belief that the Israelis will not risk firing a rocket into a densely populated area. The Al Aqsa Martyrs Brigade has agreed, and when we meet there, they even helpfully suggests that, when the interview is over, I might like to leave the building first. There is much laughter at that one.

Hamad says that he is prepared to carry out a suicide-bombing operation at some stage in the future, but he respects the decision of his leaders not to launch such attacks at the moment. Even if he didn't, I wouldn't expect him to tell me otherwise. He wouldn't be offered up to me for an interview unless he was a man who toes the party line. But why had he volunteered to kill himself and others in the first place? 'I did not volunteer.' he says. 'They asked me to make the martyrdom operation, and I said yes. What else can I say? I am a fighter. I joined the resistance. Many times I said I will do this thing.' The screening process would have been lengthy and quite systematic. The group needs to be satisfied that the volunteer has the self-control and the intelligence to get around the Israeli-army checkpoints. He would need to find his contact inside Israel and make his way to the selected city. If something went wrong, would he still be able to make his way to the target or switch to another one. And did he have the courage to go through with the attack?

First, Hamad has to be mentally prepared. 'When I am suitable, when they say I am ready, they tell me it will be soon,' he tells me. 'But they do not say when. Then they tell me it will be tomorrow.' Mohammad is given time to record a video message and make his final arrangements. He could not tell his family, and he had no job to quit. He had no last will and testament to write, but he did have a little time to think and to pray. Given what he was about to do, he probably had too much time to think.

The night before the operation, Hamad told his parents that he was staying with his married brother, who lives in a village close to where Hamad lives. 'Then I went to a safe place and stayed for the night. One of the other fighters came here too, and we stayed until early in the morning. I did not sleep. I did not *want* to sleep. I was afraid that I would not wake up. Then, another man came here and brought the bomb belt. It was then that we got the telephone call to say that the Israelis were waiting for me.'

They were waiting for you? I ask. 'They were everywhere,' he says. 'We do not use a road where there is a checkpoint usually. We take a different way: on the small roads and over the hills.' I ask him about his potential victims. But he recites the usual mantra: 'We do not wish to kill civilians, but they kill our people and we have to fight back.' I tell him that I understand that, but what about the innocent people, the women and the children he was about to kill. Had he thought about them? 'No, this is not what we are told to think about,' he says.

But you are human, I say. When you go to an Israeli street, won't you see a young Israeli girl and think that she is like your sister or your daughter? 'I do not know,' he says, 'because I did not see them.' And then the usual attempt to move away from the question. 'Why do you not ask the Israeli soldiers, the ones who fly the F-16 planes, do they not see our sisters or our daughters?' I tell him that I will ask the Israelis these questions but I want to know what he thinks. Does he hate the Israelis so much that he can't see them as people any more? 'I do not hate them,' he says. 'I hate the leaders. I do not hate the people' It's the people you are trying to kill, I say. But he does not answer.

I try again. Could you have looked these people in the eye and then killed them? 'The Palestinians have lost many, many people,' he says. 'My family, every family here, has had someone killed by the Israelis.' And suicide attacks will make their families feel better? 'No, that is stupid. Nothing makes that better. But the Israelis must know what it is like or they will not stop.' Has it worked? Have they stopped? 'No,' he says.

I ask him about the ceasefire and about the attempts to restart the peace process. He says he thinks that the Saudi Arabian plan, which calls for a full Israeli withdrawal to the pre-1967 lines, is a good one but believes that the Israelis will not accept it. I ask him why not. 'Because they will not agree that the refugees can go back to their homes,' he says.

Hamad's family are refugees. They fled what is now Israel in 1948 and moved to the West Bank. When Israel invaded the West Bank in 1967, they fled again. Now they are living in a refugee camp. 'Maybe we will be refugees again,' he says, 'this time because of the wall that the Israelis are building. We cannot live like this. But how can we go now? We have nowhere else to go.'

Then he tells me what happened to him a few months before the planned suicide bombing. 'One day I want to go to my cousin, who lives in a village near here. It is not far. But when I get to the checkpoint, the Israeli soldier says no, you cannot go. He does not look at my ID. He just says no. So I ask him why. And he just says to me "Fuck off or I will shoot you." But I will not go. I stand there and I look at him and I see he is from Russia. Then a car comes to the checkpoint and the one driving is from the settlements. And I hear him talking, and he is an American.

'So I am thinking the first one is a Russian and he is living on my grandfather's land that they took in 1948. And here is this one from America, and he lives on the land they took from my father in 1967. And why can they do this? Because they are Jewish. But I am not Jewish, so I must live in a [refugee] camp with a wall around me. So now I ask you, you think this is justice?'

So this is why you decided to become a suicide bomber? 'No. I told you, I was asked, and I said yes because there is no life here. We cannot live like this. How can we live like this? The animals will not live like this. And the world says: make peace with the Jewish [*sic*]. They tell us to live with the Jewish [*sic*]. Where? Where can we live?

So it is better to be dead? And to kill some Israelis as well? 'Not better to die than to live. But if I live like this, I will die anyway. The Israelis will kill me. Even before I try to make the suicide operation, they will kill me. Maybe in one week. Maybe in one year. But I will die. So for me it is better to die like this.'

*

Mohammad is right to be scared. The Israelis have a long memory and a long reach. They could kill him at any time, and anywhere. According to the Israeli human-rights organisation B'tselem, between the end of 2000 and the beginning of 2007, the Israeli security forces assassinated 210 Palestinians it said were militants. In the course of those operations, they also killed 128 innocent bystanders. Human-rights organisations usually refrain from referring to the latter category as 'innocent' because it implies that the actual targets of the attacks were guilty of something. Although they may have been, they were never tried or convicted. In the eyes of the law, they were innocent. Yet they received the death penalty.

Israel defends its policy of assassinations by saying that the targets are so-called 'ticking bombs': that they are actively involved in the planning of an operation. Much of the information on the identities and whereabouts of the people targeted in this way by the Israeli government comes from Palestinian informers, whose reliability and motives are extremely suspect. Israeli human-rights organisations have petitioned the High Court in Tel Aviv several times to rule on whether the killings are unlawful. But as recently as late 2006, the High Court ruled in the government's favour, accepting its argument that, once there was 'good information' and provided 'the decision to kill was taken at the highest level' – in other words on the orders of the defence minister or the prime minister – then the policy was legal. In short, the High Court ruled that Israel had to defend itself and sometimes must take extraordinary measures in order to do so.

The Israeli security forces and the government spokespeople refer to these assassinations as 'targeted killings'. The suggestion is that they are pinpointed operations in which only the person who is target is killed. The deaths of 128 bystanders indicate otherwise. For every two people targeted for assassination, another one is killed because he or she happens to be in the wrong place at the wrong time.

In one of the latest killings, Bushra Breghish, a seventeen-year-old girl, was shot dead in her bedroom as she studied for her exams. The Israeli sniper who killed her was apparently part of a unit which had been sent in to arrest her brother. According to her family, all she was holding in her hands when she was killed was a school book.

At the beginning of 2002, I was in Ramallah reporting on the Israeli incursions into the West Bank which were to culminate in the invasion called 'Defensive Shield'. The suicide bombings were approaching their zenith, and the assassinations of suspected Palestinian militants were happening on an almost-weekly basis. On a small side road near Al Bireh, we were reporting on the previous night's fighting when there was a loud explosion close by.

I looked over just in time to see a car engulfed in flames shuddering to a halt about halfway down the road. A second car, travelling in the other direction, was also on fire. As we raced out onto the road, dozens of people were gathering around the two vehicles trying to pull the victims from the flames. They managed to get two people out of the second car, but the first, which was the 'target', was an inferno. A rocket or shell had hit the first vehicle and, when it exploded, the passing car was hit by a sheet of flames.

The 'target' was a man called Abu Quaik, a local Hamas activist. The Israelis had been trying to kill him for some time for his alleged involvement in the planning of suicide bombings. But Abu Quaik was not in the car that day: it was being driven by his wife as she collected their three young children from school. The other car was also driven by a woman taking her kids home from school. Six people died that day: Abu Quaik's wife and three children, aged seven, four and three, and the second woman, who was twenty-nine, and her five-year-old daughter. Her two other children were badly injured.

By the time we arrived at the scene, the flames were so intense that you could not see inside the cars. Bits of clothing and school books had been blown out onto the road and were burning there. My cameraman, Tariq, had to put down his camera and turn away. Through the long lens of the camera, he had seen right inside the cars. I wasn't surprised when he quit the business shortly afterwards.

A rocket fired from a Apache helicopter is the usual method of assassination. Sometimes it's a bomb dropped from a fighter plane. In July 2002, the Israelis used a one-ton bomb to kill Hamas leader Salah Shehade in Gaza. They got him. But they killed fourteen other people too, most of them women and children, when the bomb hit the apartment block where Shehade was living.

In May 2001, the Israeli army tried to kill Mahmud Abu Hannoud, a Hamas activist who was in a Palestinian jail in Nablus. The Israelis were afraid that Abu Hannoud was about to be freed, so they dropped a bomb from an F-16 on the police station. Abu Hannoud escaped the blast, but eleven Palestinian policemen were killed. After that, few Palestinian policemen were willing to risk their lives by taking part in operations to capture Hamas militants.

The Israelis don't always use the crude methods of mounting rocket attacks or dropping bombs to kill their targets. One of the first assassinations of a militant Palestinian leader was that of Yahya Ayyash, the number two man in the Izz El Din Al Qassam Brigade, the military wing of Hamas. In 1995, Ayyash was high on the Israeli hit list for his role as a senior bomb-maker for the group. Ayyash was not just a manufacturer of crude bombs; he was also capable of making sophisticated devices. Israel had tried to kill him on a number of occasions, and had failed. In August 1995, during a halt in attacks by

Hamas following pressure from the Palestinian Authority, Ayyash moved to Beit Hanoun in Gaza. The Israelis knew that he phoned his family every Friday. Eventually, they recruited a collaborator whose nephew had access to Ayyash's mobile phone. They placed fifty grams of explosives and a tiny detonator in the earpiece. That Friday, as Ayyash called his father, an Israeli team, after confirming that it was his voice, triggered the device from an overhead helicopter.

The militants became very wary of using cell phones. In 2001, Iyyad Mohammad Hardan, an activist with Islamic Jihad, was so paranoid about cell phones that he refused to use one. He began to make his calls from public phones. A collaborator tipped off the Israelis, and the next time Hardan went to a particular roadside phone box, a remote-controlled bomb exploded, killing him instantly.

The use of collaborators is crucial to the 'success' of these missions – which might explain why the Israelis get it wrong so often. Frequently, their information is out of date or simply inaccurate. The Israelis need their tip-off man on the ground to identify the victim and to determine whether there are other people with him. In a moving car, that information can be out of date in about thirty seconds.

The first assassination of this intifada was the killing of Hussein Abayat from Bethlehem. He was killed in Beit Sahur in November 2000, just after the outbreak of fighting, when three rockets hit his car. Two bystanders were also killed. Both were women in their fifties. One had ten children, the other seven.

Booby traps are another favourite of the Israeli hit squads. It could be a bomb under a car. Or in the headrest. One Palestinian militant bought a model aircraft by mail order from Tel Aviv, thinking that he could modify it to carry explosives. When he received the parts, the Israelis had already made their own modifications, and it blew up in his face. As the Palestinians became more desperate for weapons, they became less careful about how they got them. Collaborators passed on booby-trapped weapons to militants, who lost an eye or a hand when they used them.

The booby traps allow the Israelis to deny any responsibility for a particular attack. The Israelis like to call these attacks 'work accidents'. The belief is that, when the Israelis deny involvement in a particular incident, it is either to protect an informer or because the killing has not been authorised.

There was no doubt that the Israelis had carried out the attack on the Abu Quaik family in Ramallah that day. They admitted it. They said that Abu Quaik's wife and children were not meant to be in the car. They said they were sorry. Two days later, a rabbi in one of the settlements said that Israel should not apologise for the deaths because the intended target was a terrorist. His comments sparked off a debate within Israel about the policy of assassinations.

For some Israelis, the practice is deeply troubling. Apart from the fact that innocent children were being incinerated as they were driven home from school, the Israeli army, and the defence minister who authorised the attack, had become jury, judge and executioner. Israel prided itself on being a democratic country – the only one in the region, as government spokespeople are keen to point out – with respect for the rule of law. How could it justify these killings? There was also the moral question: Israel was a Jewish state, so didn't it also have a moral obligation to respect human life?

Whenever an assassination takes place, 'security sources' 'reveal' to the media that the dead militant was 'a senior figure' within a certain group. The dead man is sometimes called 'a terrorist mastermind'. The same sources say that the militant killed had been responsible for planning 'a series of attacks on Israeli cities'.

No evidence is ever offered, but most of the Israeli press lap this information up and repeat it without asking for proof or further details. Some newspapers don't even report where the claim comes from but simply repeat it as if it were fact. Most Israelis believe their army when they say that it is killing only militants. And, the line runs, if mistakes are sometimes made, this is regrettable but unavoidable.

The other argument used in support of the targeted-assassinations policy is the deterrent effect. If the militants feel that they are in the cross-hairs of the Israeli special forces every time they go outside their door, then they are less likely to risk getting involved in planning further operations. 'Forcing them to keep their heads down' is the way the Israeli military people describe it.

But the effect is limited. The killings may eliminate some of the leaders of the Palestinian bomb squads, but they also help the armed groups to recruit yet more volunteers for suicide bombings and other operations. This approach by the government also bolsters support among ordinary Palestinians for the so-called 'martyrs'. Leaders of the Palestinian militant groups believe that the tactic goes beyond prevention, or deterrence, or even revenge. They see it as a deliberate provocation, aimed at drawing them into open conflict with their much-stronger enemy.

Palestinian moderates say that the killings represent an attempt by the Israeli security forces to inflame the situation and then use the resulting violence as a pretext for a planned, large-scale incursion. Several times, unilateral ceasefires which had been called by Palestinian militants collapsed after their members were killed. Many Palestinians and even some Israelis believe that right-wing elements in the Israeli security forces are operating to their own agenda.

The Palestinians try to counteract the use of informers by imposing the death penalty on anyone who is caught passing information on to the Israelis. Sometimes this takes the form of a kind of trial under the Palestinian Authority's crude judicial system. More often, it involves a kangaroo court set up by the militants themselves. Those suspected of being traitors are beaten or tortured until they admit to their 'crime'. Then they are shot. A number of times, suspected collaborators were set upon and beaten to death by angry mobs. In Ramallah, two men were strung up and hanged in the centre of the city after vigilantes beat 'confessions' out of them.

The Israelis still manage to recruit people. Very often, the collaborators are people involved in petty crime – and sometimes not so petty. The Israelis will sometimes turn a blind eye to the activities of drugs dealers in return for some information. But very often it starts with something small. A man with a permit to work in Israel is told that his documents are being cancelled unless he passes on some details about one of his neighbours. He is told that all he has to do is make one phone call. But one call soon becomes two, and before long he is a regular informant. Then he is told that, if he stops providing information, not alone will he lose his permit but the secret police will let everyone know that he has been working for them. The security forces have also been known to use blackmail, sometimes filming people in compromising situations.

4

'WE ARE ON THE SIDE OF GOD'

During the American Civil War, Abraham Lincoln was asked whether God was on the side of the Confederates or the side of the Union. 'I am not sure,' he replied. 'All I know is that we are on the side of God.' You won't get that kind of equivocation from a Jewish settler in the West Bank: God is on their side. In fact, they are there with His explicit imprimatur. This argument is virtually impossible to counter because it is so strongly held.

In 1967, after army intelligence signalled that the Jewish state was about to be attacked by its Arab neighbours for a second time, Israel launched a series of pre-emptive strikes, and in just six days it had captured the Golan Heights from Syria, the Gaza Strip from Egypt, and East Jerusalem and the West Bank from the Jordanians.

Until then, Israel's religious leaders had been less than enthusiastic about the creation of a Jewish state. Given the largely secular ideology of Zionism's founding fathers, the religious elders were doubtful whether the enterprise would be worthwhile. The Six Day War changed all that. Having been faced with what they saw as possible annihilation, the religious leaders became gripped with a messianic fervour, which resulted in a massive drive to settle their people in the Biblical homeland of Judea and Samaria, otherwise known as the West Bank. They believed that redemption would come as a result of a Jewish state being created in all of the land between the Dead Sea and the Mediterranean.

There were two other factors which led to the drive to create Jewish settlements in the land captured in 1967. The first argument was that moving Jews into these territories would provide Israel with a kind of security buffer zone. The settlers would be the first line of defence against further attacks, or could at least provide an early-warning system. The other belief was that creating these so-called 'facts on the ground' would provide Israel with bargaining chips. If and when the Israeli government ever came to negotiate with the Arabs, they could exchange land for peace. If no negotiations ensued, then they could simply hold on to the land.

But there was another powerful motive behind the policy of establishing settlements: pure territorial conquest by capturing and colonising more land. Successive political leaders subscribed to the idea of establishing 'Eretz Israel', a greater Israel. For them, the settlements constituted a land-grab pure and simple.

These were reasons enough for a majority of people in Israel either to go along with the plan or to do nothing much about stopping it. Governments from the Left and the Right went ahead with getting as many people into the settlements as possible. Successive governments didn't just allow settlement to happen, they *made* it happen. They offered every possible encouragement for people to settle in these newly captured territories.

Realising that there were not enough ideologues or zealots to populate the hills of the West Bank to the extent that they wished, successive governments drew in secular Israelis with offers of cheap housing and generous tax breaks. The greatest level of growth in the number of settlers was in the years following the signing of the Oslo Peace Accord in 1993.

In that peace deal, the Palestinians had fatally allowed the issue of the settlements to be put to the end of the long-term negotiations. Ten years later, they were nowhere near final-status negotiations, but the number of settlers had doubled. The Israeli prime minister who helped create the greatest building boom in the settlements was the left-wing Labour Party leader, Ehud Barak.

There are now more than 450,000 Jewish settlers living in the lands captured by Israel in 1967. Almost half of them are in neighbourhoods of East Jerusalem, where the Palestinians had hoped to establish the capital of their new state.

Some settlers still proffer the security argument to justify their existence. They claim to be there to make life safer for the Israelis living behind the 1948 border, the so-called Green Line. Few people accept this argument now, though. If the Palestinians wish to attack Israel proper, they just go around the settlements. This is what they have been doing for the past seven years. And it is now widely accepted that the presence of the settlements is, in itself, a provocation to the Palestinians. The settlers simply draw fire on themselves and on the soldiers of the IDF who have to be there on a permanent basis to defend them.

The notion of the settlements being bargaining chips has also been largely dropped. Look at how powerful the settlement movement has become, and how difficult it was to remove just a few thousand settlers from Gaza and a small section of the

West Bank in 2005. These people are not going anywhere: a few small settlements may be sacrificed in some further peace deal, but the vast bulk of them will stay. The Israeli government's case is that these settlements have become a de facto part of Israel. These settlements are not just a few Nissen huts on a hillside: they are cities and towns, with factories and schools, and people who have put down roots. The PLO has privately accepted this but cannot say so, because they hope to get something in return for their acceptance of some of the settlements.

Patrick Groome lives in the West Bank settlement of Ofra, just a few kilometres from Ramallah. In many ways, he is about as Irish as you can get. Reddish hair, a milky-white Celtic complexion completely unsuited to Middle East sunshine, and an Irish accent as strong as the day he left home more than twenty years ago. He even has a dog named Guinness. But Patrick is Jewish. He is an Israeli citizen. And he is a settler. He came to Israel for the first time in 1979 and worked for a while on a kibbutz in the south of Israel, not far from the Gaza Strip. Patrick was given a job in the fields, helping to grow potatoes from seeds imported by the Israeli government from County Donegal.

He fell in love with the country. And he fell in love with a local woman. Deciding to stay, Patrick joined the army and became the only Irish Catholic in the Israeli Defence Forces. He served with the Nahal Brigade, one of the elite units of the Israeli army, and spent most of his time in the Gaza area, which was under full occupation at the time.

Deciding to convert to Judaism, he went to a rabbinical court in Tel Aviv, but the rabbis told him that he was not eligible, and advised him to go away and study the teachings of the Torah. He tried again some years later, this time in London, but once more he was refused.

By this time, Patrick's first marriage had broken down, and he married for a second time, this time to Shulamit, a Canadian-born Jew he had met in the army. They went to live in Montreal, where a local rabbi helped him finally to convert to Judaism. It was the end of a very long and very difficult process. There was much to learn and to understand. And there was the very painful experience of being circumcised at twenty-six years of age. 'When you have gone through all of this, you feel that you have never been anything else except for Jewish,' he told me. 'I really felt as if I was returning to my roots.'

Patrick was born a Catholic and practised that faith until his teens. He attended a secondary school in County Offaly which helped to prepare young men for becoming members of the Franciscan Order. Did he ever entertain the notion of a life in the Franciscans? 'There were moments when, yes, I did feel that this way of life might be for me,' he says. But his faith lapsed altogether, and until he converted to Judaism, he was neither one thing nor the other. Of Catholicism, he says now that 'It's just an offshoot of Judaism, and it's an offshoot that's not in the right direction'.

The Groomes went back to Israel, but in 1991 – by which time they had two small children – they decided to try living in Ireland for a while. Patrick was appointed to head up a small unit attached to the Israeli embassy which aimed to create links between Ireland and Israel, and in particular to promote business between the two countries.

There were not exactly close ties between the two countries at the time. Patrick puts that down to a couple of factors. 'I think the anti-Jewish thing in Ireland was quite prevalent at the time, and it remains so,' he says. The other influence was what he calls Ireland's 'sympathy towards the Palestinian people, which was understandable given Ireland's own history'.

It was at this time that the full weight of Patrick's conversion to Judaism came back to haunt him. In 1994, when he was working in Dublin, his father died. His father, who was from Kildare, had been a Catholic all his life, and Patrick faced the dilemma of how to be involved in the church services. He went to a rabbi and got some advice. In the end, he felt that his faith would not allow him to attend the Catholic services, so he went to the removal but stayed outside the church. When his family, his mother and six brothers and sisters emerged from the church, they found Patrick outside, wearing his *kippa* (skullcap) and reciting from a Jewish prayer book. 'It didn't go down well,' he says.

But what happened the next day was worse. At the funeral, Patrick felt that he had to decline the offer to carry his father's coffin. And at the burial, Patrick believed that he should not be at the graveside, so he stood well back. For some members of his family, this was too much. More than a decade later, half of them still do not speak to him. He hasn't seen them in years. But he has no real regrets about what he did that day. 'No, I don't, I did what I believed to be right,' he says. 'In 1979, I made my bed, knowing full well the consequences of the steps that I took, and I am happy to remain like that.'

Two years after this, Patrick and Shulamit returned to Israel and decided to live in the West Bank settlement of Ofra. He has been there ever since, working as a teacher in the local school, and is now the proud owner of an olive grove covering about an acre and a half.

'We chose the West Bank settlements because they observe Jewish law,' says Patrick, 'but also because we thought it was important to support the ideology' of settling Jews throughout the West Bank, which Patrick and his family call 'Judea and Samaria'. It is, Patrick admits, as much a political statement as an expression of faith. 'That's what being Jewish is all about,' he tells me. 'It is a nationality and a religion.'

Patrick Groome says that he is just a 'little cog in the wheel' and is 'playing his part' in moving the Jewish project forward. 'Where it is all going to end I do not know,' he says. 'But where we all would like it to end is where the Messiah or the Saviour will arrive and we will all go up [to heaven] together.' And does he believe that the presence of settlers in the West Bank is helping to bring about that day? 'I do indeed. I really believe that we have a purpose here, and that's it.'

We talk a little about the prospects for peace. I put it to him that the settlements represent a serious obstacle to peace: the more land the settlers take, the less there is for the Palestinians. What are they supposed to do with a disjointed series of enclaves making up something less than 20 percent of the land? How can they make a country out of that? That's not the issue, he says, because it's not about the size of the country. 'Look at Luxembourg or Switzerland: they're among the smallest states in the world.' Fair enough.

So would Israel be prepared to swap its 80 percent share for the Palestinians' 20 percent? No, they would not, he responds. But the Jews might be prepared to swap some land in Israel in return for the West Bank land on which the bulk of the settlements are built. This idea has been floated before, but the land Israel was talking about – an area located close to the Gaza strip – was of very poor quality in agricultural terms. The deal would work only if the Palestinians got twice or three times as much land as they gave up, to compensate them for the loss of good-quality land and a plentiful water supply.

Either way, says Patrick, Israel is not willing to give up much of the West Bank. 'We are not going back to the old 1967 lines,' he tells me. 'The larger settlement areas, and East Jerusalem, are not negotiable.'

So where are the Palestinians to live? Patrick begins talking about how large Jordan, Saudi Arabia and Egypt are. He's suggesting that the Palestinians should move there. I put it to him that the Palestinians, who were born in what is now Israel, seem to have far fewer rights than, say, a Jew born in Russia, who can come and live anywhere they like in Israel. Why is that?

He answers: 'Because the Arabs who lived on this land, most of them were transient and they never really had rights. Some of them do have the proper documentation to prove that certain tracts of land are their property, and if that's the case, we should apologise and get out of there, but most of it [the Arab claims to land] are lies, damned lies and nothing more.' This is a statement commonly made by settlers. The Israeli government says the same: it claims that most of the land upon which the settlements are built is 'state land'.

But this is hugely disingenuous. It is 'state land' because the Israeli state declared it to be 'state land', having taken it out of private Arab ownership in the first place. According to the Israeli human-rights group B'tselem, 'declaration of land as state land has, since 1967, been the principal method used by Israel to take control of land to build settlements and create land reserves for their future expansion'.

The law that allows Israel to do this dates back to 1858, when the Ottomans ruled over Palestine. After the Turks left, the British incorporated the law into their Mandate Legislation. The Jordanians, during their rule, and the Israelis now, manipulate that law for their own purposes.

Under the legislation, a person may acquire ownership of farmland and register it after working it for ten consecutive years. Many Palestinian farmers did this. However, if the person ceases to work the land for three consecutive years, the land is considered state land, and possession is transferred to the government. According to B'tselem, between 1979 and

1992 about a quarter of a million acres of land in the West Bank was registered as state land under this system.

From the time the state begins to seize the land, the Palestinian farmer has forty-five days to appeal. B'tselem says that 'often, primarily in the 1980s, the notice of declaration of land as state land did not reach the Palestinians, and when it did, the time for filing had already passed'. Even if they did receive notice, few Palestinian farmers have the money to engage a lawyer. If they are lucky, a Palestinian NGO or an Israeli human-rights group will pay. B'tselem says that, in many cases, the Israeli government passed the lands on to settlers even before the forty-five-day period had ended.

But that's not all. Even if the land was legally declared state land – which it wasn't – then the land is supposed to be public property. It rightfully belongs to the lawful residents of the West Bank. Instead, the Israeli government, in handing it over to the settlers, 'acted improperly', according to B'tselem, 'because it administered the state land in a discriminatory and illegal manner'.

This law, and Israel's use of it, is one of the reasons why the route of the so-called 'security barrier' or 'wall' is so significant. The wall – which in some sections is actually a fence – is being constructed deep inside the West Bank. In addition to the thousands of acres of Palestinian land being seized for the construction of the barrier itself, thousands of acres of Arab land now lie on the Israeli side of the barrier. Following a lengthy series of court battles, the Israelis agreed to place a series of gateways in the barrier to allow the Arabs access to their lands on the other side. But it doesn't always work. The gates are not always open, and farmers often have no idea when they will be open or closed.

Moreover, there are very few gateways, and those that do exist don't allow the farmer direct access to his land. His land may be just the other side of the wall, but the farmer may have to make a journey of several kilometres just to get to a gate, then wait for an hour to get through, and finally travel the same distance back just to get to his fields. Frequently, farmers will make the journey only to find the gate closed, with no indication as to why, or when it might be opened.

The problem is particularly acute during harvests, when the farmers and their entire extended family need to get to the lands at specific times. If they cannot get through, they lose the harvest. The Palestinians believe that an attempt is being made to get them to leave their land untended long enough for the Israelis to declare it state land and then seize it.

The Israelis sometimes refer to the wall as a security fence or 'the separation barrier'. According to a report drawn up by the Israeli human-rights group Bimkom, or Planners for Planning Rights, some 250,000 Palestinians have been shut off from the rest of the West Bank by the 'separation barrier'. The group say that there are now about twenty-one enclaves in which the Palestinians are on the 'wrong' side of the wall. Some eight thousand people are trapped in so-called 'seam enclaves' – meaning that they are trapped between the wall and the old green line, leaving them in a virtual no man's land.

According to Bimkom, the Palestinian areas are in some cases fenced in on three sides, cutting them off from urban centres, sources of livelihood, and social services. All of this is 'severely harming daily life to the point of disintegrating Palestinian society in the area'. The report highlighted the plight of families whose homes are now cut off from the village or town in which they live. They are now effectively guests in their own homes, in that they are allowed only 'temporary residence' in this newly rezoned area. For this, they must have a permit, which has to be regularly renewed. If they don't have a permit, they are subject to heavy fines and or a jail sentence of up to five years.

For everyone caught in these newly created ghettos, medical care in the case of an emergency is a major problem. They cannot cross into Israel because they are not Israeli citizens and would require special passes. If they need help at night, or at certain times of the day, they cannot get into the West Bank, because the few gates on the wall are locked.

This means that they have to call the Israeli army and plead for the gates to be opened. If it's a medical emergency, a delay of this nature could be the difference between life and death. Bimkom outlines how, despite the Israeli High Court's ruling that the route of the wall had to take into account the 'humanitarian needs' of the Palestinians, its course was still driven primarily by the needs of the settlements. One example was the Palestinian village of Bartaa, where the route of the fence was moved almost two miles into the West Bank in order to facilitate the settlement of Rihan and the creation of a new settlement called Rihanit, leaving the people of Bartaa stranded.

Another example is the village of Bir Narbala, near Jerusalem, which has become a ghetto in which some 15,000 people are surrounded on all sides by the fence, with only one underground route in or out, which is blocked by a checkpoint. Bimkom argues – as does every other organisation which has looked objectively at this issue – that the long-term continued existence of these Arab communities is 'doubtful'.

The settlers and their supporters lobby hard to make sure that the route of the Wall considers their interests above those of anyone else. When it comes to government approval, they are pushing an open door. The route of the barrier is clearly dictated not so much by security considerations as by the desire to create open spaces between the Wall and the nearby settlements. These 'open spaces' are to become building sites for the existing settlements – the ones Israel intend to hold on to.

Ofra, where Patrick Groome and his family live, is not among these settlements. It is on the east side of the wall – the Palestinian side. If a peace deal is ever done, Ofra will probably be sacrificed. Does Patrick ever see a day when there will be a Palestinian state, and would he welcome it? 'No, I wouldn't, and no, I don't see it [happening],' he replies. 'The reason it won't happen is not because of what we [the Israelis] are doing to stop the emergence of a Palestinian state. We are not doing anything to stop it. As a matter of fact, our government has been doing everything to encourage and promote the establishment of a Palestinian state. But the Palestinians themselves are stopping the creation of a state. And the main reason they will never be able to establish a state is because they are not a nation. They don't have what it takes to be a nation.'

What does he mean by this? 'I mean they are a hodgepodge of people. A group of various people thrown together to establish a state is not going to do it. They must have a common and a fundamental, deep-rooted adherence to a certain group of values and a history. And they don't have it, because there is no such thing as a Palestinian.'

I tell him that a little over two hundred years ago there was no such thing as an American nation either, just a hodgepodge of people from all over the world. 'Ah yes,' he says, 'but they put something together and they developed something.' And the Palestinians can't do likewise? 'I do not see it, no,' he says.

'And I would not welcome it, because if there is a Palestinian state, I would lose my home and my community.'

But what hopes for peace can there be if there is no Palestinian state? Can the Arabs and the Israelis live in peace? 'I don't think we can live in peace with a state or without it,' he says. So will the occupation just continue indefinitely? 'What occupation?' he says quickly. 'There is no occupation. There is a conflict, and the land is in dispute.'

What about the Israeli High Court's reference to the Israeli military presence as a 'belligerent occupation'. Didn't Ariel Sharon himself refer to it as an occupation? And what about the illegality of the settlements: the fact that international law clearly forbids the occupying power from moving its civilians into occupied territory?

We are now back to where we started. God is the answer. 'For the people who live here, there is a law higher than that,' says Patrick. 'It is the law of God. And what counts is his law, and the belief that this is what he wants us to do. The State of Israel is not just the State of Israel. Israel is far above international law. And that's why I am here.'

5

FACING DOWN THE SETTLERS

All this talk of God's law leaves me a bit bewildered. Thinking about the settlers' use of the divine-intervention argument makes me wonder why any God, in his infinite wisdom, would bother to allocate specific pieces of real estate to one particular tribe. Chosen people or not, why would it matter to God where they live, providing they live according to His law?

The settlers may have profoundly held values, but it is obvious that waving the bible around as a title deed has no place in twenty-first-century conflict resolution. How can their needs be accommodated without destroying the legitimate hopes of the Palestinians to create a viable state of their own? The short answer is: they can't.

The settlers have to be faced down, as they were in Gaza. They have to be told to get out. The international community, if it is to have any credibility at all in defending the rights of the Palestinians and in creating a just solution to this conflict, has to insist that the settlers are in breach of international law. They will have to be given time to move, and if Israel wishes to give them new homes and lands inside Israel and compensate them for moving, then that's their own business.

But that's probably not going to happen. US president George Bush, in a speech in 2004, said that, in any peace deal with the Palestinians, Israel should not be expected to evacuate the main settlement blocs. At the time, Bush was supposed to be a kind of honest broker, driving a peace process called the Road Map, in which the issue of settlements was to be negotiated by the two sides. The Palestinians have already indicated a willingness to allow the main settlement blocs to remain, but they want something in return: if not a land swap, then some additional concessions on one of the other issues.

But here was the president of the United States, with one brash statement, sweeping the Palestinians' bargaining chips right off the negotiating table. And he didn't stop there. Bush also said that the Israelis should not have to accept the Palestinians' claim for the refugees' right of return to their former homes. This represents another rejection of international law and UN Resolutions.

The EU (who, together with the UN, Russia and the United States, made up the so-called Quartet which had drawn up the Road Map in 2003) lodged a strong protest with the Americans over Bush's comment. The White House issued a hasty statement saying that, of course, the issues of settlements and refugees were questions for the final-status negotiations, and the president did not wish to prejudge the outcome of these talks, and so on and so forth. But the damage had been done.

Ariel Sharon, who was prime minister at the time, had received the clear support of the US president for Israel's position: there would be no American pressure on Israel to make concessions on these two key issues. And the Bush statement sent a very clear message to the settlers' movement and its political supporters that, when the time came, the bigger the settlements were, the less likely it was that anyone was going to order them to be removed. The tenders for the new building work on the settlements went out the following week.

Even when an American administration tried to do something to stop the illegal settlements, Israeli ignored it. In 1977, US president Jimmy Carter requested that then Prime Minister Menachim Begin freeze the settlement programme. The basis of Carter's objection was twofold. Firstly, that the settlements greatly diminished the possibility of reaching a two-state solution, and secondly, that Israel, by moving its civilian population into occupied territories, was clearly in breach of international law, specifically the Fourth Geneva Convention (Article 49, Paragraph 6).

Israel's response was that the Geneva Convention was not applicable because the lands in question were previously held by Jordan and Egypt, which were not the sovereign powers. Carter's legal adviser rejected this, saying that the law was still applicable because protecting the interests of the ousted sovereign was not the law's 'sole or essential purpose'. Its paramount purpose was 'protecting the civilian population of an occupied territory and reserving permanent territorial changes'. The settlements were clearly there to stay, and there could be no question that they were in any way helping the Palestinians. Quite the contrary, in fact.

At the time of the Carter request, there were already 50,000 Israelis living in annexed East Jerusalem, but there were only 7,000 settlers living in the West Bank and Gaza. Not only did Begin refuse the Carter request, but he also adopted the plan of then Agriculture Minister Ariel Sharon for further growth. Sharon's plan then was to have two million Jews living in the occupied territories by 2000. That plan has failed, but twenty years later the Israelis had managed to place 7,000 settlers in Gaza alone, and a further 250,000 in the West Bank. East Jerusalem accounted for another 200,000.

The purpose of the Sharon plan was clear: it aimed to pre-empt the possibility of any territorial division of the land and to kill off any hopes of the creation of a contiguous Palestinian state. At the time, the chairman of the World Zionist Organisation's settlement department, Mattiyahu Drobless, spelt out the situation: 'The disposition of the settlements must be carried out not only around the settlements of the minorities [the Palestinians] but also in between them.'

Americas attitude to the settlers changed when Ronald Reagan succeeded Carter as president and declared that the settlements were 'not illegal'. Subsequently, American administrations declined to take a position on the legality of the settlements, preferring instead to refer to them as 'an obstacle to peace' and then doing little to stop their expansion. Israel was therefore able to keep deferring the issue, saying that it would be part of any negotiations on a final peace deal, but all the while continuing to expand the developments.

By the time Bill Clinton led the Camp David peace negotiations in 2000, Clinton's proposals for the borders of a Palestinian state had to take into account the facts on the ground. Scores of smaller settlements would go, but the larger blocs, which had been built on, or exerted control over, some of the best land in the West Bank, would have to stay.

At the time, however, the Americans did lay down one clear instruction to the Israelis. While existing settlements would be allowed to 'thicken' to allow for what was called 'natural growth', there were to be no new settlements in the West Bank. This was a key element in the first phase of the Road Map, and one which Sharon had agreed to, in theory at least.

New settlements were popping up in the West Bank all the time. Israeli left-wing groups like Peace Now reported that new outposts were being established in the remote hills. Eventually the Americans demanded to know what was going on. Sharon admitted that the new settlements were illegal under Israeli law and pledged to remove them.

Under international law, all the settlements are illegal, but the Americans accepted this artificial distinction, and asked for only the new settlements to be removed. Months later, however, the number of new outposts had continued to grow. So the Americans asked again, a little more firmly this time. Israel's reply was that there were legal complications: they could not simply order the police and the army bulldozers in to topple the houses and caravans.

The Americans asked for a full investigation into the 'illegal outposts', to determine what connection they had to the settler movement generally and what, if anything, the government had done to remove them – or, as it turned out, facilitate them. A woman named Talia Sasson was appointed to investigate. What she discovered was hardly surprising.

Sasson found that not only was the government failing to remove these settlements, but that officials within various Israeli government departments, including the housing and defence ministers were conspiring to spend tens of millions of dollars in state funds to help build illegal new settlements.

According to Sasson's report, everybody knew a little about what was going on but no one office or body had gathered all the relevant information about the illegal outposts. She found that part of the information was accessible but that 'a major part of it is concealed'. She concluded that officials must have been either completely negligent or utterly stupid not to have known what was going on. When she began to ask the officials questions, they either refused to meet her or wouldn't give straight answers to her questions.

The Ministry of Housing and Construction told Sasson that, between 2000 and 2004, it had handed out €12 million to the illegal settlements, but admitted afterwards that the figure could have been higher. Sasson thinks that the figure is far higher. And that's just one government department. Whether the state officials funded the illegal settlements for ideological reasons, for brown bags of shekels, or for both is not fully understood. Some have lost their jobs over the affair but no one has been prosecuted.

Early in 2007, the Peace Now group petitioned the High Court to evict a number of settlers who were living in the outpost of Hersha in the West Bank. Under both international statutes and Israeli law, the settlers were there illegally. Peace Now asked that they be evicted and the houses demolished.

The settlers presented evidence that the state had taken an active role in establishing the settlement between 1995 and 2004, with the provision of hundreds of thousands of euros worth of infrastructure, including roads, sewage works, a community hall and a day-care centre. The housing ministry had even drawn up a development plan that included schools and a state-owned meteorological station.

The settlers hinted that they might be prepared to leave Hersha if the government gave them some money in compensation. They had taken this land illegally, they had illegally drawn down state funds to pay for the construction of their homes, and now they wanted to be paid to give it back. They will probably get the money. On the other hand, there is no question of the Palestinian farmers, whose lands were (and are still being) used for the settlements, being compensated.

There are political implications to all of this. The Palestinian public follows these developments closely. It is well aware of Israeli state support for the 'illegal settlements'. The message they receive is that Israel has no intention of ending a settlement project which by its very nature makes the creation of a Palestinian state difficult if not impossible.

The question of removing the 'illegal settlements' has taken on a new dimension since the pullout from Gaza with the ending of the political career of the man who planned it, Ariel Sharon. Most Israelis supported the Gaza withdrawal, if only because they thought it would bring relative peace on the country's southern border. But when the Palestinian militants continued their rocket fire from Gaza, the view was that the policy had failed. Shortly afterwards, in the summer of 2006, despite the fact that Israel had withdrawn from south Lebanon in 1999, Hezbollah launched attacks on northern Israel. The idea of further withdrawals was quickly shelved.

The new prime minister, Ehud Olmert, who had helped Sharon to develop the plan to pull out of Gaza, came under such public and political pressure after the debacle of the Lebanon conflict that he was in no position to continue with the policy of disengagement. The extent of his weakness became apparent when he gave interviews to a number of Israeli newspapers several months later.

When asked when he was going to act to remove the 'illegal settlements' – the ones that had not been granted planning permission by the Israeli state – he replied: 'It has to be part of a process in which the Palestinians fulfil their commitments. That will facilitate things for us too.' Olmert was obviously running so scared of the right wing, both of his Kadima Party and in Israel as a whole, that he did not dare move even against people who were breaking the law, unless he could deliver some movement on the Palestinian issue. He made the removal of illegal outposts conditional on the Palestinians' willingness, or ability, to end the fighting, rather than the other way around. And by allowing the settlers to continue to break Israeli law, he was also breaking a promise made by Sharon to the Americans that Israel would act against the new settlements.

*

Rabbi Arik Ascherman has been insulted, spat on and physically assaulted, and even had the lives of his family threatened, by extremist settlers. Ascherman's organisation, Rabbis For Human Rights, does the dirty job of trying to protect Palestinian farmers from the small but significant element in the settler movement which attacks and intimidates their Arab neighbours on a regular basis. For the settlers, he is public enemy number one, and more than a few of them mean it when they say they want him dead.

Ascherman, who is in his mid-forties, is from Pennsylvania and studied at Harvard. After finding Zionism, he moved to Israel to serve as a community worker in an Arab village for a year and a half. There he saw what he calls 'the costs of Zionism to others'. On the question of culpability, Ascherman quotes the Jewish theologian Abraham Joshua Heschel, who said: 'Only a few are guilty, but we are all responsible.'

Ascherman moved to Israel full time in 1994, and formed Rabbis For Human Rights, to fight what he calls the 'enormity of the injustice' suffered by Palestinians living under occupation. For a time, the high-profile campaign seemed to be having an effect. But all that was to change seven years ago. 'The outbreak of the second intifada absolutely eviscerated the peace and human-rights movements in this country,' he says. 'Particularly after the violence inside Israel, a lot of people just threw up their hands and said we are not going to be involved in this any more.'

Rabbis For Human Rights tries to recruit ordinary Israelis to join his regular protests on the West Bank. If the settlers have been harassing Palestinians who are trying to get the olive harvest in, Arik and his supporters will be there to try to help the Arabs. If the settlers have moved in overnight and torn up the Palestinians' crops, then Rabbis For Human Rights will

organise a busload of Israelis to go in there and replant
everything.

I went on one of those trips and asked Arik about the settlers' claim that all of the land on the West Bank, which they
call 'Judea and Samaria', had been given to the Jews by God. He
confirmed the biblical account, but added that 'God never said
that we had to hold all of the land all of the time'. There is also,
he says, the very pertinent the question of 'whether the Jews
are morally fit to inherit the soil' at any particular time.

Amira Hass, one of the few Israeli journalists to report regularly on what is happening in the Palestinian territories, and the
only Israeli journalist who actually lives there, has frequently
exposed the nastier side of the settler movement. Palestinian
farmers are quite often shot at by settlers. A number have been
killed, and many have been injured. Mobs of settlers, armed
with sticks and clubs, have set upon Palestinians as they try to
work their fields close to the settlements.

For security reasons, many of the settlements are situated
on hilltops; their location also gives Israel control over much of
the water supplies. These supplies are often cut off or, on occasion, deliberately contaminated. Amira Hass has reported how,
when one Palestinian community went to investigate a blockage
in a particular pipe, they found that it had been broken open by
settlers and stuffed with dirty nappies and the carcasses of
chickens. In many cases, the outflow of waste water from the
settlements is allowed, or directed, to seep down into the Arab
neighbourhoods. It is not always domestic waste, either. In
some instances, the outflow carries dangerous pollutants from
the small industries which have been established in some
Jewish settlements. A number of these enterprises are 'dirty
industries' – involving the production of materials such as

asbestos, paints and pesticides – which cannot be licensed to operate inside Israel.

The opinion polls suggest that a majority of Israelis support the creation of a Palestinian state broadly along the 1967 lines: that is, all of the West Bank and Gaza, with East Jerusalem as the capital. But as Rabbi Arik Ascherman points out: 'If you ask the same people whether they wish Israel to retain the main settlement blocs in the West Bank, they will also say yes; these two answers seem to be incompatible, and I think it is indicative of the confusion and lack of clear thinking in our society on this issue.'

Ascherman's group does not get involved in the whole argument about the legality of the settlements. His is a moral imperative, informed by his religious beliefs. 'Most Israelis have very little regard for international law on this issue,' he says. 'For them, the state is sovereign, and nobody can tell the state what to do because the outside world is not an honest broker or a judge of what is moral. There is good reason for this perception. The world has stood by when Jews were being murdered.'

There is another reason for this inaction. 'It is related to the larger issue,' he says, 'the whole issue of the intifada, the killing of many Israeli civilians, and the idea that there is no willingness on the other side to negotiate. So while Israelis say that settlers are part of the problem, they do not wish to confront them when we are under fire.'

So who are these hardliners among the settlers movement, and what are they trying to achieve? According to Ascherman, the collapse of the argument that settlements were there to provide security led to a vacuum that has been filled by what he calls 'a mixture of extreme nationalism and extreme religion'. This group now makes up what he believes to be a 'significant minority – not just a handful of people' in the settler movement.

'Some of [the settlers] will say that Arabs only understand force and there is this whole ideology that the Palestinians don't respect those who treat them nicely; they only respect those who treat them harshly,' he explains.

Rabbi Ascherman describes how, when he once went with a group of volunteers to try to prevent settlers stealing the olive harvest from a Palestinian farmer's groves, he got involved in what he calls a 'surreal theological argument about the rights of non-Jews in the land of Israel'. When confronted, the settlers finally admitted that it was not about the olives, it was about 'showing the Arabs who controls the land'.

Ascherman says that the settlers never accept his invitation to sit down and have a proper discussion. All he gets is abuse. 'It starts with the comment that you are worse than the Palestinians,' he reports. 'They say they can understand the Palestinians, but I am a traitor.'

Rabbi Ascherman says that the settlers draw their particular brand of theological argument from the writings of a number of right-wing rabbis. But he says that their ideas are reinforced by 'living in a totally closed community, where these arguments are all they hear. From a very young age, they are being fed hate.' He adds, however, that many of these settlers come from communities which have been attacked by the Palestinians and have had family members murdered. 'It is not,' he says, 'as if they do not have anything to build on.'

The most worrying aspect of the settler violence is that one of the core groups involved are the so-called 'hilltop youths'. These are mainly teenagers, who, according to Ascherman, cannot be controlled even by the settlers' leaders. These are the youths who infiltrated the settlements in Gaza prior to the disengagement in the summer of 2005 and put up the stiffest resistance, attacking soldiers and police with whatever came to hand. 'They have created a kind of Frankenstein's monster,' he says. 'These young people have been taught that they are above the law, that the world is against them but that God is on their side.'

Given the current weakness of Israel's government and the stalemate over talks with the Palestinians, it seems unlikely that there will be moves to dismantle further settlements, even smaller ones, on a unilateral basis. But the perception is that the settlers movement is preparing for such an eventuality anyway. Their resistance next time will be both political and violent.

'The conclusion that the movement reached after Gaza was that they were too nice; that the appeals to the larger Israeli public for sympathy did not really work,' says Ascherman. He believes that the subsequent battles in places like Amona on the West Bank have led the settlers to conclude that the best message to send out is that any further moves against them will lead to a 'violent mess'.

The first time I met Joe, he was pointing a revolver at my head. I had walked unannounced to the hut where he lived, and knocked loudly. When he opened the door, I greeted him with a friendly 'Shalom'. His reply was 'Who the fuck are you?' Joe was a settler living on a hillside in the wilds of the West Bank. The morning I called to see him, he thought I might be an Arab trying to kill him. I told him who I was, and then helpfully pointed out that Hamas were unlikely to knock on his door first. He laughed and invited me in for coffee but said that he would not do an interview. He told me he had a couple of reasons for not talking.

'I am here illegally,' he said. 'The government doesn't want me here. Even the settlers movement doesn't like me being here, because they say I stir things up. The Arabs want to kill me. And besides, my mom doesn't know I am here. She thinks I am at college in Jerusalem.'

I tell him I don't want to get him in trouble with his mom. As he puts the revolver away in the top of a wardrobe, I see that he's also got an automatic rifle of some kind. How many guns have you got Joe? 'Just two,' he says. 'The revolver is for personal protection. The rifle is to protect my community.'

The 'community' comprises a few other mobile homes, a few badly beaten-up cars and jeeps, a water tank, and two dogs that haven't stopped barking since I arrived. 'Pretty shit, huh?' says Joe. 'But don't you go saying that we are white trash. We are Jews and we are here to liberate our land.' Joe is from Brooklyn, and is thirty-two. He came to Israel to 'get stuck in', as he puts it.

'You think we're the bad guys, don't you?' he asks me. I say it doesn't matter what I think, the Palestinians think he is stealing their land and that he's prepared to kill them to keep it. 'You fucking Irish, what do you know about it. People have been trying to kill the Jews for thousands of years,' he says. 'But this time, we are fighting back.' I suggest that the only reason people are trying to kill him is because he is a settler on the West Bank. And he might be safer in Brooklyn. 'In Brooklyn, I didn't really know I was Jewish,' he says. 'I never went to the synagogue. I didn't do kosher. None of that stuff.' You do it now? 'Yeah, well, kinda. But what I am doing is more important in a way.'

When Joe came over to Israel, he tried to join the army, but they declined to take him. He says it was because he was too old. I think there might be another reason: college in Jerusalem was just a ruse for him to get some money from his mother. He signed up at the beginning of the autumn semester and hadn't been back since. 'A lot of rich kids from back home like to feel Jewish by studying here for a year or two,' he says, 'but they never do anything. They never come near Judea and Samaria.'

Joe came because he wanted to be 'a true-blue Jew'. His mother is Jewish but is neither devout nor nationalistic. His father, who is 'long gone', was an Italian Catholic. His brother is 'sorta Jewish'. One of his sisters is an agnostic. 'The other one is a lesbian.'

Apart from his mother, Joe hasn't had much contact with any of his family in quite some time. 'We are a totally fucked-up family,' he admits. 'I was really screwed up for a while until I found out who I was.' Joe has become a fact on the ground. 'Once we are here – once we are anywhere – we are here to stay,' he says. 'Some day this will be a town, a city maybe. A Jewish city. Part of greater Israel. I am helping to build that.'

Does he believe that this will hasten the day when the Messiah will come. 'Oh, I dunno about all that stuff,' he replies. 'All I know is that we have to live here because God command-ed us to live here. That's all there is to it.' And what about the Arabs who hope to have a state here some day? 'Look, man, the Arabs are not going to have a state here. There is no such thing as Palestine. Not here, anyway. If they want to call somewhere "Palestine", they can go over there,' he says, pointing at the hills leading to Jordan. 'There's already a couple of million [of Arabs] there anyway. Let the rest of them go there.'

Why would they leave? 'We can give them money to go. There are lots of folks back home willing to pay them some-thing like ten thousand dollars to leave here. That's a good deal for these guys. They have nothing. They will be better off.' But supposing they don't want the money? Are you going to kill them all? 'I don't want to kill anyone. I will only kill to defend myself and my country. If they attack me, I will kill them.' Has he ever killed someone? 'Maybe. Some guys, some terrorists, came around here one night a couple of weeks ago and started shooting at us. We fired back. I heard a lot of yelling. I think maybe I might have hit someone.'

I ask if he has ever taken part in any of the attacks on Arab landowners. 'We go to a bunch of Jewish communities around here to protect them. If people are worried that the Arabs are coming too close to their communities, then we go over there and move them right along.' The settlers have legally held weapons. The men organise themselves into groups to patrol the settlement perimeter, and beyond it.

The Palestinians who get 'too close' are the ones whose farms adjoin the settlements. When the farmers try to get into their olive groves or fruit orchards, Joe and his friends move the Arabs right along by firing shots over their heads. And sometimes not over their heads but into their legs. Then they destroy the groves or the fruit trees to stop the Palestinians coming back. 'It gets kinda crazy out there,' he says, 'and we have to defend ourselves. Those Arabs start throwing rocks and shit, and there's lots of them hiding out in the trees. It's dangerous. We could be shot at by terrorists at any time, so we've got to clear the area.' The idea that he might actually be provoking the trouble seems not to enter his head.

The settlers live in an area which is under military rule, which means that they should be subject to the same laws as the Palestinians who are living there. But they are not. The Arabs are dealt with in a military court. The settlers come under ordinary Israeli criminal jurisdiction. There are huge differences in the way the two groups are treated. The settlers are not held for as long before their case is heard, they have the right to talk to a lawyer immediately and in court, and they can offer fuller evidence in their defence. The starkest difference is in the maximum sentence they may serve, and the time off they are granted. In many instances, the cases against the settlers don't even go to court.

Joe's illegal settlement has about twenty people in it. Most have been there since the settlement was established a couple of years before. He is hoping for some new members to join shortly. 'It's the weather,' he says. 'It gets very cold up here in the winter, and nobody wants to live here. But now it's the spring. Look how beautiful it is. This is how it was thousands of years ago, when the Jewish people lived all around here.' I tell him it's also how it looked for the past hundreds of years, when the Palestinians farmed it. 'You don't understand. It was never their land,' he says. 'Sure, they had it, but that was because the Jewish people were driven off it. Now we are back to claim what is ours.' By what right? I ask him. 'By God's law,' he says. 'God gave the land to us. He told Abraham that this is the land of the Jews. What more do you need to know?' Nothing, really. I thank him for his time, and tell him that if his mother ever finds out where he is, it won't be me who told her.

6

No Home to Go to?

If there is one aspect of the final-status negotiations that really perturbs the Israelis, it's the question of Palestinian refugees returning to their former homes in what is now Israel. As far as the Jews are concerned, the return of the refugees would mean the 'destruction' of Israel.

The United Nations has more than four and a half million refugees registered in camps in the Palestinian territories, Syria, Jordan and Lebanon. At one stage in the recent peace negotiations, there was talk of a 'token' return of several thousand refugees over a few years. Now, attitudes have hardened, and most Israelis talk in terms of not a single refugee going home.

In fact, such is the divisive nature of this issue that the Israelis are now putting forward the argument that these people are not refugees at all. The Israelis say that only a small percentage of the four and a half million are real refugees in the sense that they were born in the former Palestine. The other 90 percent, they say, are the children and grandchildren of those who fled, and should not be included in any tally. Israeli government spokespeople now refer to the 'so-called refugee problem'.

The Palestinians insist that everyone who is listed with the UN as a refugee is entitled to that status under international law. They say that UN Resolutions recommending that they be allowed to return to their former homes give them a legal right to reclaim what is theirs. They want that right to be formally acknowledged by Israel, and they want either to return home or to be relocated elsewhere. Either way, they want compensation for their loss.

The Israelis claim that the vast majority of the 700,000 Palestinians who fled their homes during the fighting in 1948 did so voluntarily or because they were told to so by their own leaders or by the advancing Arab armies. The Palestinians say that this is not true and that, even if it was, it does not negate the legitimacy of the claim. They make the point that leaving your home to avoid being killed is not the same as leaving voluntarily.

Ahmad Abdullah Hammad is one of those Palestinians who ran for his life in 1948, and he has been a refugee ever since. Actually, he was too young to run at the time. He was carried out, as a three-month-old baby, by his fleeing mother when the Israeli forces advanced on his village of Houlayqat in the south of what was then British Mandate Palestine.

Ahmad and his family now live in Jabalya refugee camp in Gaza City. An estimated 120,000 people live here in an area of about a quarter of a kilometre square: the camp is one of the most densely populated areas on earth. Ahmad's home is slightly bigger than average by local standards, which means that he has about four rooms upstairs, and another two downstairs, for his now-married sons and daughters, and their children.

Overlooked on all sides by other apartment blocks, the flat is dark, and furnished with only the bare essentials. It is always spotlessly clean. I've been visiting Ahmad for five years or more, and if he offers food – which he has every time I've been there – I sit on the floor and he serves up hummus and vegetables, and hot sweet tea with some mint leaves.

The street outside is just well-flattened grit and sand but, given the overcrowding in the camp, it is surprisingly wide. Elsewhere, the houses are linked by narrow little pathways, but here, at the entrance to the Hammad home, is a street wide enough for three lanes of traffic. Or an Israeli tank. When Ariel Sharon was the general in charge of the Southern Command, he ordered scores of tiny houses and shops to be demolished to create a street wide enough to get his tanks down. The locals sometimes refer to it as 'Sharon Boulevard'.

This is all very different from how things might have been. The Hammad family owned around a hundred *dunams* (twenty-five acres) of land just outside the village. Some of it was pretty good land too. They grew citrus fruits and vegetables, and although they were not wealthy, they were doing all right. A few months before the fighting with the Jews broke out, Ahmad's father died of a heart attack, leaving his wife, and eight children all under the age of sixteen. Ahmad was the youngest.

But there were strong family ties in the village. Aunts and uncles and various cousins rallied around to comfort the family and help keep the farm going. These were uncertain times. Following the hasty departure of the British, the United Nations had drawn up a plan to divide the land in two in order to create a Jewish state and a Palestinian state.

Under the plan, tens of thousands of Palestinians would lose their land. But Houlayqat, where about four hundred people lived, farming around 1,700 acres, was to be spared. The village, situated about twenty-five kilometres north-east of the Gaza strip, was to become part of the new Palestinian state. Or at least that was the plan. Overall, too many Palestinians were losing out for the UN plan to be acceptable to them. There was no way that the Arabs could accept that they, as the majority population, with ownership of some three-quarters of the land, would agree to a partition plan which left them with less than half the land. Moreover, several hundred thousand of them would be caught on the wrong side of the new border, leaving them in the new Jewish state.

When the serious fighting broke out in 1948, the entire country was engulfed in the violence. The fact that Ahmad's village was in the sector earmarked for a Palestinian state did not make any difference. Soon, Egyptian forces were advancing from the south, soldiers from Saudi Arabia were moving across from the east, and the Israelis were everywhere, trying to fight on about six different fronts. The day they all converged on Houlayqat was the day all of Ahmad's brothers and sisters were killed. A tactic used by the irregular Jewish groups like the Irgun and the Stern Gang was to surround villages on three sides and send word to the residents that the Jews were advancing. At the time, word had spread throughout Palestine of the massacre of civilians in other areas. Some of these tales were exaggerated or simply made up. Others were true. When villagers heard that the Jewish militias were on their way, there was panic, and everyone who could fled south to Gaza through the corridor that had been left open by the Israelis.

Ahmad tells me that his mother wrapped a blanket around her and tucked the little boy inside, grabbed whatever valuables she had, and ran. On the roads south, they met hundreds of other refugees from the neighbouring villages. These people too had fled after fighting had spread to their villages, or after reports of massacres had reached them.

About halfway between their home and the Gaza strip, they found a place where people were stopping to rest. Everyone was talking excitedly about what was happening. There were stories of cold-blooded murder by the Jews, and tales of heroic resistance by the Arabs. The belief among most was that the combined Arab armies would drive back the Jews, and people would be able to return to their villages.

Not everyone would make it to Gaza. Some of the badly injured, the elderly, and the very young did not survive the first leg of the journey, and they were being buried there on the side of the road.

When Ahmad's mother arrived at the rest stop, she sat herself down under a tree and began asking people whether they had seen her sons or daughters, or anyone from her village. When she unwrapped the blanket, little Ahmad was lifeless.

She daubed a little water on his face, but he didn't move. She shook him gently and called his name, but there was no sign of life.

Convinced that she had suffocated her baby, she began to scream. Other women came over to comfort her, and the men came and took the lifeless child away, to be buried in a mass grave they had dug nearby. According to Ahmad's mother, the men were literally shoving dry earth onto the bodies when the little boy came to and began crying. He was hauled from the ground and returned to his hysterical mother on the side of the road. She thanked God all the way to Gaza.

Sixty years later, Ahmad Abdullah Hammad is still in Gaza. He now has eight children of his own, five daughters and three sons – exactly the same number and combination as had been born to his own mother and father. Ahmad's mother, who died six years ago, always ignored the names that Ahmad and his wife Siniora had chosen for her grandchildren, and insisted on calling them by the names of her own children. Before she died, Ahmad's mother gave her son her three most treasured possessions: a piece of cloth from the suit of her late husband, the key to their house, and the deeds to the family land. Ahmad holds them for the day when, as he puts it, he will return to claim what is his.

Ahmad recently retired from his job as a schoolteacher at a

school run by the UN in Gaza. After thirty-eight years working at the school, he receives a small pension. Siniora passed away just a few months ago. He now has eighteen grandchildren, with a few more on the way. As soon as the children are old enough to understand, he tells them about where the family came from. He tells them that the Hamad family were not always poor people living in the filth and squalor of Jabalya. He tells them about the family's twenty-five acres back in Houlayqat. He tells them about the lemon trees and the apricots and the wide open spaces where it is great to run. He tells them about going home.

After 1967, when Israel began its occupation of the Gaza Strip, it was possible for Palestinians to cross the 1948 green line if they had a permit for work. To cross over without a permit meant risking arrest. Ahmad and his mother ran that risk on a number of occasions, taking Ahmad's children to see Houlayqat. But there was no Houlayqat. It had been reduced to rubble, just like three hundred other Arab villages throughout the country. Only a few stones here and there indicated that this place had once been home to several hundred people.

That was twenty years ago. Ahmad cannot go there now because he is not allowed to enter Israel from Gaza. But he knows that there is an Israeli community living there now. They call it Helez. Ahmad has heard that there is a small oil well on part of what used to be his village. 'My dream is still to return to my land,' he tells me. 'It is still my land. I don't care what they call it now, it is still mine. I have the legal documents to prove it.' He says that, if he can't return, then he hopes at least to be buried there when he dies. 'Then my soul will be at peace,' he says. I put it to him as gently as possible that perhaps his wish is hopeless. 'I cannot live without this hope,' he says. 'My family cannot live without something to wish for. That is why we pass this hope on from generation to generation. If we lose this hope, we will lose our life.'

But what about the Israeli argument that there isn't enough room for the refugees to return to areas where six million Jews now live. 'I believe in this English saying that where there is a will, there is a way. If the Israelis want to help us, then they can help us. I don't care who lives there now. I will be very glad if my next-door neighbour is Jewish. I will be a good neighbour for him, and we will make parties together. If he is Jewish, then that is something between him and God. I am a Muslim, but we can live together. We must bury the hatchet and teach our children about forgiveness.'

Ahmad says that, if there is to be an end to the conflict, then there has to be a solution to the problem of the refugees. 'They have used my land for sixty years,' he says, 'so they should have to pay me compensation. But it will still be my land. I will not accept money in order to be told to stay in a camp in Gaza. I want to return to my land.'

Ahmad believes that the issue of the refugees is the Israelis' problem. 'The problem is [that] they want to live in a Jewish state,' he says, 'but we want to live in a secular state with no differences between Jewish and Muslim and Christian. We just want to be citizens, equal under the law.' Does he believe that there can be a peace deal between Arabs and Israelis? 'Listen to me,' he says, 'I am prepared to give something for peace. I have a hundred *dunams* [twenty-five acres] of land. I will give fifty *dunams* just for peace. I will give more; I will give up three-quarters of my land, but I must be allowed to keep some part of my land and to live there with dignity.'

Some Israelis still maintain that the vast majority of Palestinians left their homes and lands of their own accord. They will tell you that Israel pleaded with the Arabs to stay, and that it was mainly the calls by Arab leaders, both in Palestine and outside of it, which led to locals deserting their property.

Immediately after the war, this version of events became part of the official Israeli narrative. The lie was repeated time and again by Israeli government spokesmen. It was written into the history books that Israeli children studied at school. To admit otherwise now would be to make Israel legally and morally responsible for the fate of those refugees. Worse, it would give credence to the Arab claim that the Jewish state was born in sin.

Irishman Erskine Childers was one of the first researchers to investigate whether Palestinians had been encouraged to leave their lands by their own leaders. Childers spent some time in Israel in 1958, trying to find documentary evidence of the claims. Childers was particularly concerned that the Zionist version of events had been largely accepted by the international community, and that consequently there was little effort made to return the Palestinians to their homes.

Childers decided to test the undocumented charge that the Arab evacuation orders were broadcast by Arab radio, and found that the research could be 'done thoroughly' because the BBC monitored all Middle Eastern broadcasts throughout 1948. The BBC records, and similar ones from a US monitoring unit, were – and still are – at the British Museum.

In an article published in the *Spectator* magazine in 1961, Childers wrote: 'There was not a single order, or appeal, or suggestion about evacuation from Palestine from any Arab radio station, inside or outside Palestine, in 1948. There is repeated monitored record of Arab appeals, even flat orders, to the civilians of Palestine to stay put.'

The Palestinian story was that they were driven out, either by the regular Jewish army, the Haganah, or by the irregular forces of the Stern Gang and the Irgun. Sometimes they were forced out by the barrel of a gun, and sometimes under clear threats from the Zionist forces. Childers reported: 'From the analysis of only some of the sources of the Arab exodus, it is clear beyond all doubt that official Zionist forces were responsible for the expulsion of thousands upon thousands of Arabs, and for deliberate incitement to panic.'

Childers went on to say that it did not matter if some of the expulsions were carried out by the so-called irregular forces. As he put it: 'The Israeli government today pays former Irgunists and Sternists the same war pensions as former Haganah troops.'

But Israel was not responsible for all of the refugees fleeing. As the region began to drift towards war, many rich and middle-class Arabs gathered their belongings and left for other Arab nations, or for Europe. Some rich landowners even had time to sell their properties to the Jewish Agency, which was buying up Arab land on which to settle Jewish immigrants before they fled. However, the vast bulk of them left because they were driven out. It was much later, with the release of the official Israel government documents of the period, that the real truth began to come out. A number of Israeli historians, including Benny Morris, Avi Shlaim, Illan Pape and Tom Segev, began to sift through the papers, and subsequently revealed the full story.

The issue of the refugees came to the fore again recently with the revived Arab League peace plan for the Middle East. The plan, which was first floated back in 2002, offers Israel full normalisation of relations with the twenty-two Arab countries in return for a Palestinian state based roughly on the old 1948 lines: in effect, the West Bank, including East Jerusalem and Gaza. The plan calls for a 'negotiated and just settlement' to the problem. Israeli right-wingers responded by insisting that the Arabs delete that part of the plan because the question of refugees was simply not open for negotiation. In fact, according to the *Jerusalem Post* newspaper, the inclusion of the demand to negotiate the right of return made the whole deal 'a non-starter'.

Soon afterwards, in an interview in the same newspaper, Prime Minister Ehud Olmert reiterated that Israel would not accept the return to Israel of any refugees. 'It is out of the question,' he said. 'I will never accept a solution that is based on their return; any number.' And Olmert went further: he also ruled out any suggestion of Israel recognising 'a right of return' in principle as part of a deal whereby Israel would decide how many refugees could return. This was the mechanism devised by President Bill Clinton during the Camp David negotiations back in 2000. The so-called Clinton parameters included the notion of a token number of Palestinians being allowed back each year for a period of five years or so. The bulk of the refugees would either return to the new Palestinian state, be absorbed by their host countries, or be allowed to relocate to various third countries, such as Canada.

Eran Lerman heads the Jerusalem branch of the American-Jewish Committee, a think-tank and lobby group. A former army intelligence officer, he became one of Israel's negotiators for the Camp David and Taba peace talks in 2000. At his office in the centre of Jerusalem, I asked him how close the last set of negotiations had come to resolving the question of refugees. 'At Camp David they were not very close,' he says. 'At Taba, there was really nothing official. People were just sounding each other out and putting forward ideas. Yossi Beilan [the former Israeli justice minister and architect of the Oslo Accords] was floating this document which he had drawn up, but very few [Israeli] people who read the document agree with it.' Beilan's idea was that 50,000 Palestinians from the camps in Lebanon, who were generally accepted to be the worst-off of the refugees, would be allowed to return to their former homes. But doing that would mean that Israel would, in Eran Lerman's words, 'be going halfway towards accepting guilt' for expropriating Arab lands. That, he says, would run against the grain. The Israeli story that 1948 was a legitimate war cannot be altered. 'We cannot be apologetic,' he says. 'That is taking it too far. We can acknowledge, however, that they suffered.'

According to the Israeli prime minister, Ehud Olmert, any earlier proposals on the refugee issue are dead and gone. In an interview in early 2007, he said: 'I will not agree to accept any kind of Israeli responsibility for the refugees. Full stop. It is a moral issue of the highest level. I don't think that we should accept any kind of responsibility for the creation of the problem.'

Eran Lerman thinks that there is a very slim chance that Israel can acknowledge culpability. But he notes that this will not happen 'unless it is mutual. If the Palestinians are prepared to accept that they should have not begun the war, then maybe. It may sound trivial, but it is not. Once you construct Israel as a colonial endeavour, then you have pulled the rug from under the legitimacy of the State of Israel. The Jewish state and the ideas of ancestral land are undermined.'

Rabbi David Rosen, the former Chief Rabbi of Ireland, has been living in Israel for some years now. He too works with the American-Jewish Committee, and is the international president of the World Conference of Religions for Peace. I ask him about Israel's difficulty with accepting some measure of blame for creating the problem of the refugees. Could it do this, or just apologise, without somehow accepting that the State of

Israel was 'born in sin'?

'To acknowledge that there was a conflict and that people were uprooted and there was a lot of tragedy involved is, in fact, to prove that you were born in virtue and that you have the honesty to admit your mistake,' he says. 'It is those who are not willing to accept their share in the burden who are the ones who are reflecting the sin rather than the virtue. It requires a degree of self-confidence to do that.' But he adds: 'At the same time, the Palestinians will not admit to their contribution to the suffering and to the tragedies that their leadership brought upon them and us.'

UN Resolution 194 states that the refugees 'wishing to return to their homes and live in peace with their neighbours should be permitted to do so at the earliest practicable date. Compensation should be paid for the property of those choosing not to return, and for loss of, or damage to, property.' Implementation of the Resolution would not result in all Palestinians returning to their former lands, as many would not wish to. Given the choice of moving either to a free and independent Palestinian state, with adequate compensation, or living under Israeli rule in a Jewish state, most of the refugees would naturally choose the former. They have indicated as much in opinion polls. Or they would instead accept an offer of relocation to Canada or a EU country, again with compensation.

The Saudi peace plan, adopted in March 2002 by the twenty-two countries of the Arab League, calls for the 'achievement of a just solution to the refugee problem to be agreed upon in accordance with UN General Assembly Resolution 194'. According to Gershon Baskin, the CEO of the Israel/Palestine Centre for Research and Information, the key word in the Saudi plan is 'agreed'. He points out that this is the first time that an

Arab document has used the word in this context. This means that nothing could be forced upon Israel. That is not how the Saudi proposal is seen in other quarters, however. According to Caroline Glick, a deputy editor of the right-wing *Jerusalem Post*, accepting the Saudi initiative would mean Israel 'allowing itself to become inundated with millions of hostile foreign-born Arabs who call themselves Palestinian refugees'. She obviously missed the word 'agreed'.

Israel makes the point that the UN is far more generous in applying the term 'refugee' to Palestinians than other people in a similar situation. It says that UNRWA, the UN agency set up to deal with the Palestinian refugees, extends that status to any descendants of persons displaced in 1948, and points out that this is a right that is not always given to people in other conflict situations. Israel also accuses the UN of allowing the refugee problem to grow and fester for sixty years, deliberately avoiding any attempt to settle the refugees either in the countries where they now reside or elsewhere. The UN's answer is that it is their mandate to provide for the refugees until such time as there is an agreed solution to the problem: in other words, until Israel agrees a solution.

Israel also points the finger at 'host countries' like Syria and Lebanon, and says that they are deliberately keeping the Palestinians in abject poverty in the refugee camps in order to foment hatred of the Jewish state. There is some truth in this accusation. Certainly Israel's neighbours have never been reluctant to use the Palestinian situation to stir up trouble for Israel and to divert attention from their own domestic problems. But those same Arab countries are extremely wary, given their own delicate tribal balances, of trying to absorb large numbers of Palestinians.

For Syria and Lebanon, it is not a question of refusing to allow the Jewish state off the hook, just for the sake of spite. They also hope that, if they do absorb refugees, they will be able to prise some concessions from the Israelis in return. The alternative, say the Arabs, is to give up a bargaining chip in advance of any negotiations. If they do that, they say, Israel would be less inclined to compromise on the other issues.

Israel may try to deny responsibility for creating the refugee problem but it cannot deny that it is Israel's job to help solve it. And they can't do that by simply saying they will not negotiate. Without an end to the refugee issue, there can be no end to the conflict. For the Palestinians, the solution lies in Israel admitting what it did. In order to get out of this conundrum, the Israelis will have to dream up some form of words that will sound like an apology to the Palestinians – but will sound like nothing of the kind to their own public. Or they could just admit that they did wrong. Either way, it will have to be clear that the deal does not entitle four and a half million Palestinians to load up their carts and start heading for Tel Aviv.

According to Shlomo Avineri, professor of political science at Hebrew University of Jerusalem, part of the fallout of the collapse of the talks in 2000 was that 'most Israelis believe the refugee issue is not a humanitarian problem that obviously has to be addressed generously by Israel, but that it is the Trojan horse by means of which the Palestinians would undermine the existence of Israel as a Jewish state'.

Avineri, writing for the Bitter Lemons website, believes that no Israeli leader can be expected to make significant concessions on the West Bank and plan the evacuation of tens of thousands of Israeli settlers when he cannot reassure his public that, if Israel gives up the territories occupied in 1967, the Palestinians will see this as a final and unambiguous end of the conflict. In other words, that the fear among many Israelis is that the Palestinians will seek the return of millions of refugees to Israel, thus starting another war.

What needs to happen, according to Avineri, is for a Palestinian leader clearly and unequivocally to give up the refugees' right of return to Israel, but not to a future Palestinian state. Then, he says, the Israeli public would put enormous pressure on its government to take what he calls the 'dramatic leap towards defining the final borders of Israel'.

But as he says himself, the hope that some Palestinian leader will do this is 'utopian'. Palestinian leaders have made the right of return a rallying cry for the resistance for sixty years. For them to give up this demand now would amount to political suicide. In fact, they would probably be shot within days.

No one wants to tell the Palestinian refugees that they are not going home. Not after all the misery and heartbreak they have experienced. Yasser Arafat, the master crowd-pleaser, always told them that they would be returning any day now, when he should in fact have been preparing them for the awful truth that they would never be going back to their ancestral lands. He could have let them down gently and given then new hopes of being well compensated and living happy lives in an independent Palestine, in downtown Toronto, or on a little patch of land in County Leitrim. But Arafat ducked the issue, and none of the current generation of Palestinian leaders dares to raise it.

Like their Israeli counterparts, the Palestinian leaders will have to be able to talk of major gains elsewhere before they even mention the subject of refugees. Returning from the talks and admitting that they got nothing on refugees – not even an apology – is not an option. Any Palestinian leader negotiating a deal on independence will have to obtain firm guarantees on issues like Jerusalem and the dismantling of settlements before they can even broach the possibility of the refugees not going home. It doesn't help their cause when the Israelis are saying that the question is not even up for discussion. For the Palestinian leadership, coming back from talks without a good deal on refugees is one thing. Going there having agreed to exclude the issue from the outset would lead to the collapse of the negotiations on day one.

7

'GUEST OF THE NATION'

Before becoming refugees in Aruba camp, near Hebron, the Ja'ara family owned land in what is now called Beit Shemesh, a Jewish area on the Israeli side of Jerusalem. Jihad Ja'ara still calls the area by its Arab name, Deir Aban. 'I will never agree that this is not my land,' he says. 'I will agree for this time to have peace, but I would never give it up. We can return some day.'

Jihad Ja'ara shuffles around the kitchen of his neat little semi-detached town house in Sutton in north Dublin, making coffee. He still walks with a slight limp, a result of the Israeli bullet which shattered his leg during the siege of the Church of the Nativity in Bethlehem five years ago.

I suggest to him that if millions of refugees are allowed to move back to Israel, this would effectively mean the end of the Jewish state. His reply is that by bringing Jewish people to the Middle East from all over the world, the Israelis are destroying the potential state of Palestine.

Since the end of the Bethlehem siege, Jihad Ja'ara has been a refugee in Ireland. The Irish government agreed to take two of the militants who had been holed up in Manger Square in a deal to end the thirty-nine-day standoff at the church. If it had not been a church, the Israeli army would have gone in after them. But this was held to be the birthplace of Christ, and the international community could not allow a bloody fight to the death there. Even the Vatican got involved, and applied considerable pressure on both sides to end the siege peacefully.

In the end, the deal allowed the militants out. Some of them were then illegally deported to Gaza. The others, including Ja'ara, who was brought out of the church on a stretcher after sustaining a gunshot wound, were flown first to Cyprus and then taken to a number of other EU countries that had agreed to receive them.

When the Israeli forces attacked Bethlehem in 2002, it was part of the 'Defensive Shield' operation, which followed a spate of suicide bombings inside Israel. As a senior leader of the Al Aqsa Martyrs Brigade, Jihad Ja'ara was on the Israelis' wanted list.

'When they attacked Bethlehem, we tried to defend the city,' he tells me. 'They were using tanks and heavy weapons, and we had very little to fight back with. We withstood [them] for three days, but after that we had no ammunition.' As the resistance crumbled, men began to run towards the church buildings in Manger Square. 'We did not have a plan to go to the church,' he claims now. 'It was the only safe place to be. We believed that this is a holy place and that they cannot attack us here. But they tried.'

Jihad Ja'ara says that he did not set out to become a Palestinian militant. Before the intifada broke out, he was a policeman serving with the Palestinian Preventative Security

Services, established as part of the Oslo Peace Accords to maintain law and order in the occupied territories.

But the way he tells it, he could never have been anything other than a fighter, 'because I grew up in a camp [Aroub refugee camp, near Hebron] and saw the terrible things the Israelis do. Even the games we play as children are about the fighting between the Israelis and the Palestinians. It is like learning a language. Every day you see blood. That is our life. And you start to ask why these people are doing this to us. And bit by bit you start to think about fighting them.'

When Jihad was thirteen, he was sent to jail for seven years. 'I was stone-throwing with lots of other kids,' he remembers. The young boys from the camps would line up on a hill over-looking a road linking Jerusalem with the Jewish settlements in the south and throw stones at the passing cars. 'By accident, my stone hit the windscreen [of a car] and the man driving crashed the car and died,' he remembers. He served the full seven years in a number of different Israeli jails, where he met many influ-ential leaders of the resistance. 'They educated me about the struggle, it was my university,' he says.

When he was released, it was the mid-1990s and the first intifada was over. The PLO had signed the Oslo Accord with Israel, which gave the Palestinians limited self-autonomy in some areas, with the promise of more to come. When the deal began to unravel, Jihad Ja'ara was serving with the Palestinian security forces in Jericho.

As part of the Oslo Accords, there were attempts to set up a number of joint business ventures between Israelis and Palestinians. One of the more bizarre ideas was the opening of casinos in the Palestinian town of Jericho. Israel had, and still has, very strict laws relating to gambling, so a number of Jewish business people, some with links to Ariel Sharon and other top

Israeli politicians, came up with the bright idea of turning the sleepy desert town of Jericho into the Las Vegas of the Middle East.

A number of the Palestinian partners were members of the newly founded Palestinian Authority. They had just returned from exile in Tunis to take the plum jobs in the administration, and there was much grumbling among ordinary Arabs that the new, self-appointed leaders already had their noses in the trough. Worse, they were already doing business with the old enemy. But the when the money started rolling in, the people of Jericho at least were grateful enough for the jobs and the money, and said nothing.

For a while, the thing worked. Jericho is less than an hour's drive from Israel, and even closer to Jordan, where many rich Arabs hang out. So there were plenty of people from both sides willing to forget about old enmities and get on with some serious hedonism. But when the second intifada broke out, the casinos were forced to close.

As increasingly angry Palestinians took to the streets, policeman Ja'ara and his colleagues were given the job of protecting the premises. On 30 September 2000, the day that Mohammad Dura, a twelve-year-old Palestinian boy, was killed in Gaza, the place erupted. Television pictures of the little boy cowering behind his father, desperately trying to take cover where there was none, were beamed around the Arab world. The Israelis were blamed for the boy's death, and the killing spread.

When the clashes between Israeli troops and Palestinian youths began in Jericho, Jihad and the other members of the security forces didn't know how to react. Jihad was under orders to guard the casino and not to get involved in the clashes. A seven-year-old boy issued him with new orders. 'This kid was

111

standing right beside me when the shooting started,' he remembers. 'When the Israelis killed the first Palestinian, the boy said to me: "I am ashamed of you. You have a gun and you do not protect us. You do not fight for your home." I told him to shut up.' Then a second Palestinian was killed. Again the young boy began to shout at the bewildered Ja'ara. The third person to be killed was a friend of Jihad's. 'After that, I had two choices: join in or do nothing. I put the boy behind me and started shooting.'

I ask him whether he killed any of the Israelis in Jericho. 'Maybe yes,' he says. 'It was war. They shoot at us, we shoot at them.' Jihad claims that he had had no prior involvement with the militant groups, but from then on he was involved, and the Israelis had him on their wanted list. At best, that meant life in jail; at worst, it meant he would be killed. 'After what happened in Jericho, they tried to assassinate me three times,' he says. Jericho is too small a place for a wanted man to hide: Jihad fled to Ramallah. He hid there for six months, but the Israelis had pursued him and were trying again to kill him. Eventually he was forced to take refuge in the Muqata, the headquarters of Yasser Arafat, in Ramallah.

There were dozens of others like him hiding out in Arafat's compound at that time. The Israelis ordered the Palestinian president to stop harbouring the fugitives, or face the consequences. Word spread that the Israelis were preparing to come into Arafat's compound after the men. Under cover of darkness, the Palestinians slipped out and dispersed throughout the West Bank. Jihad decided to head for Bethlehem.

'I took my gun with me because I said to myself: if they catch me, I will not give myself up, I will fight,' he remembers. 'I walked for three nights over the mountains, and eventually got to Bethlehem with the help of some friends.' Even there, he was not safe. He claims that on a number of occasions, the Israelis tried to kill him. By then, Jihad had become a leader of the Al Aqsa Martyrs in Bethlehem. The first attempt on his life there was when Israeli soldiers opened fire on the house where he was staying.

The second attack was a bit more sophisticated. Ja'ara was trying to buy a second-hand car, which had come into the West Bank after being stolen in Israel. Sometimes the car was stolen with the owner's cooperation. An Israeli wishing to get rid of an old car and claim on the insurance would simply tell the criminals where the car would be, and then keep out of the way. The car would then be stolen, and delivered to Palestinian criminals on the border or seam line.

But Israeli intelligence got in on the act by using the Palestinians involved in these activities as informers in return for the Israelis turning a blind eye to the operation. When the Israelis heard that Jihad Ja'ara was in the market, they seized their chance, intercepted the car and planted a bomb inside it. The device was remotely controlled, to be triggered when the proud new owner took it for a – very short – test drive. But the car was stopped by Palestinian police, who quickly spotted the booby-trap device. It was a narrow escape, but the Israelis were not about to give up.

By then the Israelis wanted Ja'ara for more than just the Jericho incident. According to Israeli security sources, he was responsible for the killing of two Israeli soldiers while he was in Jericho: one on the day of the incident at the casino, and another one month later, before he fled to Ramallah. They also wanted him for planning a suicide bombing in Jerusalem. On that occasion, in March 2002, a car carrying a woman suicide bomber blew up prematurely on the way to a shopping centre.

When we met, I asked him about the extent of his involvement in the fighting. He admitted being behind what he called 'the explosion inside Israel'. I also asked him about the claims made in a book written by *Newsweek* magazine's Jerusalem bureau chief, Joshua Hammer. In the book, *A Season in Bethlehem*, Hammer gives a detailed account of the siege of the Church of the Nativity and the events leading up to it. One of the key incidents he describes was the killing of an American Jew named Avi Boaz, who had been living in Jerusalem but spent time in Bethlehem, where he had some business dealings.

Boaz, a seventy-year-old New Yorker, was seized in Bethlehem by members of the Al Aqsa Martyrs Brigade in January 2002. He was then led away to a quiet part of town and shot dead. The militant group claimed that the elderly American had been involved with Israeli intelligence and had passed on information about the movements of militants in Bethlehem. They also claimed that he had been part of a business consortium building illegal Jewish settlements in Har Homa, a valuable piece of land just outside Bethlehem which had been expropriated from the Palestinians.

The Israeli security services say that Boaz's car had been riddled with automatic fire. According to Hammer, Jihad Ja'ara was directly involved in the seizure of Boaz. He claims that Ja'ara was present at the killing but did not actually open fire himself. The journalist quotes Ja'ara from an interview he conducted with him some time later in Dublin. In the interview, Ja'ara clearly puts himself in the frame.

'This is all just lies,' Ja'ara told me when I read the quotes out to him. Did you kill Avi Boaz? 'No, I did not kill him.'

Were you there when he was killed? 'No.' So why does Joshua Hammer report that you admitted involvement in the attack? 'I don't know why he would write these things,' he says. 'If I was involved, I would not be so stupid as to admit it.' At the time of my interview with Ja'ara, in May 2007, there were moves by the American authorities to have him extradited to face charges in connection with the killing of Boaz, a US citizen.

'This is not the first time that I have been blamed for this killing. That information is coming from the Israelis, but it is not true,' Ja'ara says. He claims not to have known Boaz, but he knew that the American was involved in the building of the settlement outside Bethlehem. Did that make him a 'legitimate target' in the eyes of the Al Aqsa Martyrs Brigade? 'If somebody killed him, I am sure they had a good reason' is all he will say.

But why does he think he is being put in the frame for the killing? Ja'ara thinks it may be because of accusations which have been made by another member of the Al Aqsa Martyrs Brigade, Riad Al Amur, who is serving life in prison for the killing. 'You know how the Israelis can get people to say things when they are in prison' is his explanation.

Hammer also quotes Ja'ara as admitting being involved in the killing of a number of Palestinians accused of acting as informers for the Israelis. Again, Ja'ara denies all responsibility for these deaths. 'That is not true,' he says. 'It is true that these people [those accused of being collaborators] were killed,' he says, 'and it is true that they helped the Israelis to kill the Palestinian fighters, but I am not saying that I killed them.' But you think that collaborators should be killed? 'Of course' is his reply.

Joshua Hammer, who has since left Jerusalem, stands over his account of his meeting with Ja'ara. By telephone, he tells me that he had not recorded the interview but had taken careful notes. He remembered being surprised by how forthright the former Al Aqsa member was about his involvement.

Since Ja'ara's arrival in Ireland, Israeli government sources have been telling reporters that Ja'ara is still involved in organising violence back home. I ask him whether this is true. 'Even George Bush didn't like the fact that I was here,' he says. 'The Americans tried to put pressure on the Irish government to have me thrown out, but I respect this country and I respect the law here. I did not do any wrong in Ireland.'

Maybe so, but are you still involved? 'I never forget Palestine,' he says, 'and I will never forget my people, and that's what I told the Irish security. They knew when I came here that I was a leader of the Al Aqsa Brigade. I said that I will still work with these people. I will respect your country and do nothing wrong.'

How does he feel about being called a terrorist? 'For me, I don't care. I trust myself. I believe in what do, and I am always proud of what I do and of my people. If I had not done what I did in Jericho, I would never have forgiven myself for betraying my people when they were dying.'

I ask him about the type of operations he was involved in back home and why they targeted civilians rather than just the military. 'From what I believe, all the Israelis are army' is his reply. 'They do not have civilians: they all carry guns and kill Palestinians.' I tell him that this is obviously untrue. What about children? 'If my children do not have a life, then the Israelis must not have a life' is his answer.

Do you hate all Israelis? 'I hate Israel, I do not hate the Jewish people,' he says. 'I hate the people who occupy my country. I would hate them even if they were Irish. I do not hate them because they are Jewish. There is a big difference. The problem between the Israelis and the Palestinians is not about religion. We have no problem with the Jewish religion. We have a problem with the Israelis because they kill our people and take our land.'

I ask whether one of the results of this killing of civilians, apart from the misery it causes, is the creation of more hatred on the other side. Does the killing of civilians not alienate ordinary Israelis who might otherwise support an end to the occupation? 'The Israelis must feel for the Palestinians' mothers: if we are not safe in our houses, then they should not be safe. If my people are dying, they must die. I do not care.'

Ja'ara believes that peace with the Israelis is possible if they end the occupation and allow for the creation of a Palestinian state on the land they seized in 1967, including East Jerusalem. In addition, he wants all of the Palestinian prisoners (about ten thousand men, women and children) released, and an agreement to allow all of the refugees to return.

But what about all the settlers in the West Bank? 'They must leave, even if there is one million of them. That is, if they want to live in Israel. If they want to stay where they are, under Palestinian rule, they are welcome. That's their problem.'

And you think all of this is possible in the near future? 'One day we will have our freedom. We are not expecting it now. I read Irish history: Ireland did not get theirs for eight hundred years, so in the same way one day we will get ours.' And how will that be achieved, by politics or fighting? 'It doesn't matter. It has to be real politics. For now, the Palestinians can try politics, but behind the politicians must be the freedom fighters. They [the politicians] must have the power and the support of the people and the resistance.'

Can you understand why the Israelis might be reluctant to allow the creation of a Palestinian state right now? 'It's because they think that the Palestinians believe that if they get the 1967 land, then tomorrow they will want more. But that's their problem.'

Can you convince them otherwise? 'What I teach my children is that all of Palestine is for the Palestinian people, but we are prepared to make peace for a long time. I would agree to take the 1967 lands now, but maybe after a long time, after one hundred years, we will get all our lands back.'

And in that scenario, what would happen to the Jewish people? 'That would be up to the people then to decide.' But in the meantime, you are prepared to recognise the State of Israel? 'If we make peace with them, then we agree that they have a state' is his answer. This acceptance, he says, is similar to that of the

Irish republicans who made a peace deal with the British but still pursue the aim of a united Ireland.

Do you think you will ever be allowed to leave Ireland and return to your home. And if you do go back, do you still fear being killed? 'From the moment I joined the resistance, I know that one day I will be killed. If I ever go back, they will try to kill me. I believe there was a plan to kill me here in Ireland but it was prevented by the Irish security services. This is what I was told.' But that is a report no one is likely to confirm.

8

'WE ARE FIGHTING FOR EVERY STONE HERE'

The French-run Secours Catholique operates out of an imposing old stone building just beyond the Mount of Olives in East
Jerusalem. Its grounds cover the side of a hill, and from the
carefully cultivated gardens you can view the entire city of
Jerusalem. In the middle distance, three sides of the walled Old
City can be seen. Father Michael O'Sullivan enthusiastically
points out the holy sites inside the walls. Over there are the two
domes of the mosques built on Haram Al Sharif, in front the
Western Wall, or Wailing Wall. Beyond that, to the right, he
directs my gaze to where the Church of the Holy Sepulchre is
clearly visible above the flat roofs.

From the roof of the building, he points out where the
Jewish settlements have begun to appear here and there. The
gleaming new buildings, and the presence close by of heavily
armed Israeli troops, stand out among the grubby old structures of the Arab population. As Israel extends its power over
this half of the city, Father O'Sullivan tells me he believes that
the future of Arab East Jerusalem is very bleak.

'I only see an Israeli Arab East Jerusalem, because if the present Israeli policies continue, then it will be totally cut off from its natural hinterland in the West Bank, and the only option for the Palestinians living here will be to swallow the Israeli pill and have Israeli nationality forced upon them. Many people have already done so. It's a submission to the status quo: they have no other option.'

When the Israelis illegally annexed the city, the annexation expanded Jerusalem's so-called municipal boundaries. The government drew up new maps and planned new developments, to give the political act some tangible expression. New settlements were built, roads were opened up, and whole areas on the eastern side of the city became Jewish neighbourhoods. About two hundred thousand Israelis now live in parts of East Jerusalem which were seized from the Arabs in 1967. There are so many of them, and they have been there for so long, that where they live – places like Gilo and Talpiot – are no longer referred to as settlements. Even when many of the foreign media refer to numbers of settlers, they mention the 250,000 who are living illegally in the West Bank. Most do not include the Israelis who are living in East Jerusalem. To all intents and purposes, the line between East Jerusalem and West Jerusalem has become harder to distinguish than ever before.

Born in Kilrush in County Clare, Father Michael worked in Arab North Africa for a decade before coming to the Holy Land. He is a member of the White Fathers Order, attached to Saint Anne's Church, a beautiful twelfth-century church in Jerusalem which was built by the Crusaders, and he is director of Secours Catholique, the French Caritas.

Father Michael is, quite literally, in a great position to view the changing character of East Jerusalem. As the Palestinians are gradually being pushed out of the centre of the city,

Jerusalem is losing its Christian as well as its Muslim population. And as the Israelis and the Palestinians jostle for position here, the institutional Christian churches are stuck in the middle.

When the original plan for the partition of Palestine was drawn up sixty years ago, the idea was that Jerusalem would remain an open city, to be shared by the two nations and all three religions. It is nothing like that now: Israel's consolidation of its power following the illegal annexation in 1967 has resulted in the city becoming not just less Palestinian but less Muslim and less Christian too. At the same time, the rise of a more radical, fundamentalist Islam amongst Palestinians is adding to the pressure on the Christian community.

'The Christian community in Jerusalem is a community that is in the process of disappearing,' Father Michael tells me. 'That's due in the main to the occupation and to the economic situation which has imposed itself because of the occupation. Today, you have only between five and seven thousand Christians, divided up into fourteen different churches, and that's significantly down from even a few years ago.'

Apart from the Armenian population, the Christians see themselves as essentially Arabs, and they have sided with the Muslims in the political process, despite the friction between the two faiths. Traditionally the merchant classes, the wealthier Christians have been among the first to leave Jerusalem. 'Many of them have been educated in Christian schools in Europe,' says Father Michael, 'and they have seen and got used to a better life, so they are emigrating.'

Those who cannot afford to leave the country are being forced further East. 'The Arab population is being squeezed out because of the Wall and the building of the settlements in East Jerusalem. Because of this, the normal hinterland of the West Bank cities of Ramallah and Hebron and Bethlehem is no longer accessible from here. Instead of travelling in and out, they tend to move there,' explains Father Michael.

*

When the Israelis annexed East Jerusalem and its environs in 1967, they incorporated some 200,000 Palestinians into its jurisdiction. The Palestinians were offered Israeli citizenship but, not surprisingly, they declined. They saw accepting Israel citizenship as bowing to the occupiers and not just accepting the annexation but giving it legitimacy. They were issued with the so-called blue ID cards, making them 'permanent' residents of the Israeli state but not citizens. They paid their taxes to Israel, and in theory they could benefit from Israel's social welfare system, including state-funded hospitals and schools, but in practice what they were able to access was the inferior end of a clearly two-tier system.

In theory, as residents of Israel they have access to Israel, but increasingly the practice is that they don't have the same freedom to travel as Jewish Israeli citizens and are being increasingly enclosed in Jerusalem. Some of them have opted to move temporarily to Ramallah to try to find work, but if they are found to be living in the West Bank they are deemed to be West Bankers, and their East Jerusalem ID is taken away from them. This means that they lose their social-security benefits, their children's allowances and medical care, and so on. Because of the restrictions on their movements, most Jerusalem Arabs rarely get to see their family members on the West Bank. If they have family in the Gaza Strip, they may never have seen them: travel to the Gaza Strip is completely forbidden. For the Christian Arabs, there is the further problem that they do not have access to the holy sites in Bethlehem. Similarly, people in Bethlehem can't get to Jerusalem.

As a result, more and more Palestinians are giving up their status as permanent residents and quietly opting for Israeli citizenship. 'Many of them say that they would prefer to be Israeli citizens, even living in an illegally annexed East Jerusalem, rather than be subject to the near-anarchy of a practically non-existent Palestinian entity on the other side,' explains Father Michael.

For the various Christian Churches in East Jerusalem, it is becoming increasingly difficult to keep their institutions running smoothly. Bringing in foreign priests is a slow and problematic process. The Churches have to apply to the Israelis for visas for the priests to come and work in East Jerusalem. Those Churches who draw members from neighbouring Arab countries, like Syria or Egypt, or even Jordan, find it especially difficult to get visas. Denominations with European staff find things a little easier.

The new Jewish settlements that Father Michael was pointing out to me on the roof are the cause of much friction with the local population, and with the various Christian churches. 'There is daily tension between the settlers and the religious institutions because some of our lands are up for grabs,' explains Father Michael. 'Some churches sell buildings and lands because they need the money. They may sell directly to the settlers or they may sell to a third party, who in turn sells it on to the settlers. Plus, there are problems with the registration of lands because the papers go back generations, and so the pressure increases on the Churches to sell up.'

Given that most countries view the Israeli annexation of East Jerusalem as illegal, you might think that strenuous efforts would be being made to end it, or at least to curtail its effects. Not so, according to Father Michael. 'There is this sense that we have been forgotten,' he says. 'The international community is not seen to be doing enough to highlight the injustices done by the occupation of East Jerusalem, or indeed to the rest of the Palestinian territories.'

He continues: 'Even within the Vatican, traditionally seen as supporting the Palestinian cause, there is a generation of leaders which is suffering some kind of guilt complex because of what happened during the Second World War, and the same is true of certain European governments.'

Father Michael does not claim that there is an attempt by the Jewish state to 'squeeze out' the Christians from Jerusalem. However, he says that 'Whether one likes it or not, there are many Jews or Israelis who see Christianity as a thorn in their side. I suppose they see it as a bit of a sect. Some Jews have said to me that they respect Jesus but that it's a pity that the whole thing happened. In a sense, they were saying that the establishment of Christianity was a mistake, and so our holy places are also a mistake, and must take second place in the chosen land of the chosen people.'

There may not be a state-sponsored effort to marginalise the Christian Churches, but there are wheels within wheels, and the various state organisations have an agenda of consolidating Israel's hold over East Jerusalem, and elsewhere in the Holy Land. 'At the moment, the Israel parliament approved a move that would put a footpath all around the Sea of Galilee, which is about sixteen or seventeen kilometres of a walkway,' says Father Michael. 'For us, the Sea of Galilee is a holy place. It's a place where a lot of the ministry of Jesus Christ took place, and we are certainly not in favour of turning it into an ordinary beach. Now, some of the western side of the Sea of Galilee is owned by the different Churches, and we are engaged in a big battle to reverse this decision.'

Another example of the pressure on the Christian Churches is what is happening at the Church of the Holy

Sepulchre in the Old City. The church has been given special status, which means that it is supposed to be exempt from the usual by-laws. 'The Israelis have come and put security cameras all around this shrine, which again is not respecting that special status,' Father Michael says. I ask him what future Christianity has in the land of its birth. 'We are fighting for every stone and every square metre of land here,' he replies.

'E1' is the name of the latest and biggest settlement project in East Jerusalem. At the time of writing, the construction had been suspended after objections from several European governments, including Ireland. Even the Americans, who have in recent years done almost nothing about illegal Israeli settlements, have come out against this project. That's because, if it goes ahead, E1, which is situated between Jerusalem and the existing colony of Ma'aleh Adumim, will become the final brick in a wall of settlements separating East Jerusalem from the West Bank. Worse, it will cut the West Bank in two, dividing it into two separate cantons, one to the north and one to the south of Jerusalem. How the Palestinians might be expected to travel up or down the West Bank if E1 goes ahead has not been explained. At best, they will use underground tunnels.

A vast area of land has been cleared for the building of E1. The original plan was to erect 3,500 housing units. That plan is now on hold due to opposition from the Palestinians and foreign governments. But right in the middle of this space, a four-storey police station has been built. A four-lane highway is being constructed through the middle of the site. And E1 has been declared to be on the Israeli side of the Wall, or security barrier. In short, the project may be 'on hold', but there is little doubt about Israel's intentions to proceed with it as soon as it can.

A similar process is under way further inside East Jerusalem. A housing estate is going up here, a block of apartments there: this creeping colonialism has continued for decades, to the point where Arabs are being slowly squeezed out of more and more areas. The settlers' plan is eventually to join up these 'facts on the ground' and complete the removal of the Arabs from these areas.

Very often, these moves are not fully appreciated until it is too late: that is, after planning permission has been granted and the building work has begun. The extent to which Israel is prepared to ignore international protests about the legality of the settlements was hammered home with the attempt to demolish the Shepard's Hotel in the Sheik Jarrar neighbourhood of East Jerusalem and build apartments for more than a hundred families of settlers. The new settlement was to be situated within fifty metres of the British Consulate in East Jerusalem. The British lodged a complaint with the Israelis on the grounds that the settlement would not only change the Arab character of this sensitive area but also pose a security risk to its consulate. The outcome in this case has yet to be decided.

Most Arabs are extremely reluctant to sell their property in East Jerusalem to Jews. They know that an Israeli who wants to buy there is likely to be either a settler or a representative of the settlers movement. Arabs who sell to settlers are frequently attacked, and their homes set on fire. A number of them have been killed. In some cases, Palestinian landowners have pretended that they did not know the true identity of the purchaser when they were selling their land. Usually, when a Palestinian sells to a settler, he has already left the area before the transaction is discovered.

It is not just ordinary Palestinians who are feeling the squeeze as Israel continues its drive to alter the demographic balance of the eastern half of Jerusalem. The Greek Orthodox Church has been in the Holy Land for more than seventeen hundred years. With the other Christian churches, it shares control of the holy sites in the Old City of Jerusalem. The Greek Orthodox Church is also one of the largest private landowners in Israel and the Palestinian territories. Its property portfolio includes some very valuable land in Jerusalem, and in the Old City in particular – the very land that the Israeli settlers have been seeking to acquire.

The tale of how the settlers went after one valuable Old City site is like something from the time of Florence under the Medicis. The Greeks' possessions included land – on which three old hotels stood – situated right beside the Jaffa Gate of the old city walls. On Jerusalem's monopoly board, this is about as deep a shade of dark blue as you can get.

A few years ago, the then Greek Patriarch of Jerusalem, Irenaois, granted power of attorney to a man named Nicos Papadimas to make certain transactions for the church. Nicos, who is married to an Israeli woman and, according to the Israeli press, 'loves life, fancy cars and a good cigar', was approached by an Israeli organisation, Ateret Cohanim, which promotes the establishment of new Jewish settlements in the Old City. The deal involved a long-term lease of the three hotels at Jaffa Gate to companies registered in the Virgin Islands. Papadimas signed that deal, and then another one for a second property in the Old City. Then he disappeared.

When details of the deals became public, there was uproar. The Patriarch, Irenaois, declared that he had no knowledge of the affair, but the Holy Synod of the Church voted to depose him and appointed a new Patriarch, Theophilus, in his place. But Irenaois was not about to go easily. He lodged appeals in the courts in Tel Aviv to try to stop the land deal going ahead, on the basis that the powers granted to Papadimas did not include the right to make the deal. He lobbied the Orthodox community in Israel and Palestine to support him, and in the meantime he refused to budge from his office.

So the Greeks had several big problems. Two Patriarchs. A divided community. A controversial land deal which was causing serious upset both to the Arabs and to other Christian groups. Not to mention the possible loss of some very valuable property. So the Israeli government sent in a man called Tzachi Hanegbi to mediate.

Years earlier, when he was a young student at the Hebrew University in Jerusalem, Hanegbi was convicted of assaulting an Arab student during some scuffles on the campus. He didn't just hit him; he attacked him with a bicycle chain. Hanegbi went on to become a leading member of the Likud Party and was eventually appointed as the minister responsible for church affairs in Ariel Sharon's government.

Hanegbi went to see the newly appointed Patriarch. Theophilus explained that, although his predecessor was refusing to go, he was the properly elected new leader of the Church and was seeking the necessary formal recognition from the government of Israel.

The minister explained that his government was kindly disposed towards recognising the appointment and putting the whole nasty business behind it. All Theophilus had to do was to agree to the land deal and sign the properties over to the settlers. Theophilus declared that he could not (or would not) do so, and the meeting ended. It later transpired that Hanegbi had conveyed a similar message of support, with the same condition attached, to Irenaois. Irenaois's response is not known. The saga is currently ongoing, and is now bound up in legal disputes and inquiries by government committee. There has also been a serious deterioration in the relationship between the Greek Orthodox Church and the Arab leaders. There has been one further significant development. Tzachi Hanegbi has been convicted on corruption charges unrelated to this affair, and may have to be released from jail to testify.

*

After a few years living in Manchester, Irishman Guy Gordon moved to Israel and married an Italian woman, Nicole Nitsa. Together with their four-year-old daughter Maya, they now live in the Baka area of West Jerusalem. But Guy doesn't call it 'West Jerusalem'. He calls it 'Jerusalem'. Like most Israelis, he sees Jerusalem as the permanent and indivisible capital of the Jewish state. And, like a clear majority of Jews, he is not inclined to give it up.

Guy Gordon, who is thirty-three, left Ireland in 1996. The move had been on the cards for some time. I first met Gordon's family twenty years ago, while I was making a TV documentary about the Jews in Ireland. Guy's father David told me that he was intent on taking the family to Britain because, given the size of the Jewish community in Ireland, it would be difficult if not impossible for his four sons to marry within the faith if they stayed.

'I never encountered any animosity growing up in Dublin but I always felt different,' Guy remembers. 'I felt like a Zionist and seemed to know that it was a question of when I would come here rather than if. For Guy, Israel meant 'a place which [Jews] could call their own, where they did not have to feel different or threatened, or as the guests of another people'.

Guy remembers wearing the Jewish skullcap, the *kippa*, around the streets of Dublin and being stared at. 'There was a bit of slagging,' he recalls. 'Fellas used to say "Oh here comes the Pope", but there was nothing nasty about it.' Though he has lived outside Ireland for ten years, Guy says that he keeps in touch with what is happening there. He says that he would not feel happy wearing his *kippa* on the streets of Dublin today. 'With the increasingly extremist Muslim elements who have settled in certain areas of Dublin, I would be a lot more nervous,' he says. He tells me he misses what he terms the 'gentility and civility of Irish life'. He misses, too, the warmth and friendliness of the Irish – which he contrasts with 'the gruffness and rudeness' you get from Israelis, at least at first.

Guy recalls that he was 'much more religious' when he came to Israel first. 'Now I tend to lean more towards the secular,' he says, 'but at the beginning there was a certain kind of messianic religious element to my religious beliefs. Now we are a nation like any other, and there is much more of a civic element to my Zionism than a religious one.'

Like all young Israelis, Guy did his army service, and he is still a reservist. During 'Operation Defensive Shield', the mass incursion into the West Bank in 2002, he served as a sniper with one of the IDF's elite infantry units. 'My job was to kill the bad guys before they killed us,' he says.

On the question of Jerusalem, Guy is adamant that Israel can give no quarter. He says that the Arabs can have part of East Jerusalem but that the Old City is not for negotiation. 'There are constant attempts in the Arab media to try to rubbish the Jews claim to Jerusalem,' he says. 'They try to deny our historical claim, and we have to stand our ground.'

'When it comes to the Temple Mount [which the Arabs call 'Haram Al Sharif'], there is no way that we can concede control. Some of [the Arabs'] claims for religious connection to that area are very, very specious indeed. Only latterly have these links to the site been written into their histories, only in the last century, whereas Jerusalem has been at the centre of Jewish prayer and literature and history for the past two thousand years.'

So, if you cast doubt over the validity of the Arab claim to the Old City as home to Islam's third-holiest shrine, where does that leave the Palestinians? 'Well, obviously they would have to have total access to this shrine, but we, the Israelis, certainly can't relinquish sovereignty over it. There can be no compromise on the Temple Mount.'

This raises the whole question of the Jews' biblical claim over the land of Israel – not just the holy sites but the mass of the land itself. Religious Israelis refer to the West Bank as 'Judea and Samaria': places which were supposedly given by God to the Jews. Does he agree with that view? 'I don't think it provides a basis for a political claim. But I don't think history can be consigned to the dustbin. We have a historical claim, we have a link to the land going back for thousands of years, but I do not think we have a divine right to the land. We don't own it because God promised it to Abraham. That kind of thing might warm my heart but it doesn't cut the mustard in the modern world.'

9

'WHEN JESUS CAME,

WE WERE HERE TO WELCOME HIM'

'Our family has been in Jerusalem for a very long time. We used to joke that when Jesus came, we were here to welcome him.' Terry Balata, a schoolteacher, is an East Jerusalem Arab whose family has been divided by the wall the Israelis have built in the city. For generations, members of the extended family lived close to each other in a part of the East called Abu Dis. That connection to the city was destroyed when the Israelis erected the nine-metre-high concrete slabs right behind her house and left her cut off. Part of her uncle's property was right on the route of the Wall and was demolished. Many of her family were left on the Palestinian side of the wall. Terry was stranded on the 'Israeli' side.

But that was only half the problem. When the Wall was built, Palestinians from the West Bank could no longer access those parts of East Jerusalem on the 'Israeli' side of the Wall. At the time, Terry was married to a Palestinian from the West Bank called Salah. As a result of the new dividing line, Salah was not allowed into his own house. Nor could he get to his workshop, which was also on the 'Israeli' side. His business ran into serious trouble, and he had to move to the West Bank to try to survive. Terry, as an East Jerusalem-born Palestinian, is considered by the Israelis as a 'permanent resident', a so-called blue-ID-card-holder. If she moved to the West Bank, she would lose that status, and with it the right to live in her own city. So, along with the couple's two daughters, she stayed in Jerusalem.

Under Israeli rules, Salah, as a West Bank resident, could not live in Jerusalem. And Terry, as an East Jerusalem resident, could not enter the West Bank without a special permit. She had to spend two hours crossing a checkpoint just to see her husband. 'The Israelis used to ask me about the purpose of my visits to Ramallah,' Terry remembers, 'and I would fill in the application form by writing "sleeping with my husband".' It made for an impossible life. 'The relationship was already in some trouble,' Terry admits, 'but when we could not see each other regularly, the whole thing collapsed.' The couple are now divorced.

Terry works part-time with various non-aligned community groups, and she is raising the couple's two daughters, fifteen-year-old Zena and Yasmin, who is ten. When Zena turns sixteen – which is when she will need ID papers – she will have to decide whether to live with her mother or her father. Whichever option she chooses, there is literally no going back. Under Israeli rules, she either has to be a 'permanent resident' of Jerusalem, which means that she will have little access to the West Bank, and her father, or give up that 'blue ID' and becomes a resident of the West Bank, from where it will be virtually impossible for her to see her mother on a regular basis.

In the first six years of the intifada, the Palestinians in East Jerusalem have been only marginally involved in the violence. But there have been riots when Israeli police have prevented young men from praying at the city's Al Aqsa Mosque, and that fighting became more serious when Israel attempted to carry out some construction work near the Islamic shrines.

But although East Jerusalem has not produced anything like the violence that has been seen elsewhere, Terry Balata and others have been warning for some time now that this situation could soon change. There is a growing anger among young Palestinians in the city about the fact that they are being marginalised.

'We are telling the Israelis that they need to look in particular at what they are doing in Jerusalem,' says Terry. 'They are breaking up Palestinian areas there and blocking them off from the West Bank. Life is becoming more and more difficult. If that doesn't stop, then we are very afraid that the next wave of suicide bombers will come from Jerusalem.'

For the entire Arab population of East Jerusalem, the building of the Wall through the centre of the city represents a 'lose-lose' situation. One group is caught on the Israeli side of the Wall, with little or no access to the Palestinian side of the city, or to the West Bank. The other is trapped on the Palestinian side, with the Wall in front of them, and behind them an increasing number of settlements that are gradually severing Palestinians' links with the West Bank.

The Arabs of Jerusalem who live under direct Israeli rule are getting a raw deal. About a third of the population of Jerusalem is Arab, yet, according to the Palestinian human-rights organisation Ir Amin, those residents receive only 10 percent of the city budget.

According to the Ir Amin report, there are no new municipal schools, public parks, community centres or post offices in Palestinian areas of East Jerusalem. The roads are not paved properly, garbage is collected infrequently, and there is little street lighting. The report also revealed that residents have found it increasingly difficult to reach their workplaces or to get to where they study or worship. Ir Amin say that many of the businesses in the Palestinian sector of the city have been forced to close down.

The Palestinians who live under Israeli control in East Jerusalem feel that the underfunding of municipal services is a deliberate effort by the Israelis to make life intolerable for the Palestinians. They see it as an attempt to cause the Arab neighborhoods to wither and die, forcing people to depart the capital and move to the West Bank. According to the Arabs, Israel's strategy is to keep as much of the land – and as few of the people – as possible.

It is all about demographics. The growth rate of the Arab population is twice that of the Jewish population in Jerusalem, and if there is no change in the reproduction rates, by 2035 there will be an equal number of Arabs and Jews in the city, according to research by the Jerusalem Institute for Israel Studies. Taking this into account, an American-Israeli research team has recommended that the Jewish state annex further territory in the East, according to a report in the *Ha'aretz* newspaper. The researchers say that such a move will also result in annexing a Palestinian population but claims that, if the city's municipal boundaries are not expanded, the housing and employment situation for Israelis will worsen, and more Jews will leave the city. The researchers' argument is that the Israeli-controlled portion of the city needs more space in order to prosper. In the short term, this will mean more Arabs living in the municipality, but in the long term, the area will become more attractive to Jews, and the demographics will swing back in favour of them.

It is perhaps in the tightly packed Old City of Jerusalem that the Jewish colonisation is most noticeable. The narrow old streets, surrounded by the wall built during the Ottoman rule, are the real prize for Israelis who claim that they are the only people who should be living here. The Old City has been divided up into quarters, in a process which began in 1187, when Muslim leader Saladin captured Jerusalem: one for the Jews, one for the Muslims, one for the Christians, and one for the Armenians. The last time redividing the city was mooted, the suggestion made by US president Bill Clinton was that each group would keep what they had. This may no longer be possible: in the spring of 2007, the *Jerusalem Post* newspaper reported that at that time there were eight hundred Jews living in the Muslim and Christian quarters of the old city.

'Zionism didn't end in 1948 and 1967,' Daniel Lourier, a spokesman for Ateret Cohanim, the organisation behind buying up properties for Jewish settlers in Jerusalem, is quoted in the *Jerusalem Post* as saying. Lourier is upfront about what he is trying to do. He told the BBC in 2006 that Jerusalem is a Jewish city and that Israel should stop apologising for this fact. 'We should not be afraid to say to the world that it belongs to us,' he said.

Some of the new Jewish neighbourhoods are being built right beside Arab housing. An area which the Jews call Shimon Hatzadik has a playground in an open space but it can't be used by the local Arab kids. 'The neighbourhood decided not to let them play here, so they'll know who is in charge and not give us any trouble,' said Bryna Segal, one of the Jewish-community leaders.

Silwan, an Arab area just outside the city walls, is another district that is feeling the squeeze. Karim Arafat, a Palestinian who owns a tailor shop, complains that on Jewish holidays the streets are closed off and he is confined to his home while 'the settlers dance on the streets'. He says that it is possible for the

Jews and the Arabs to live together some day but, he told the *Jerusalem Post*, 'Jews and settlers are not the same thing'. He says that he cannot live with the settlers. 'And I don't think you could either,' he told the *Post*'s reporter.

In May 2007, the Israeli bulldozers arrived in the early hours of the morning at an illegally built home for Palestinian children with special needs. According to the Israeli-run Committee Against House Demolitions, the border police knocked on the doors of the building in Wadi Joz in occupied East Jerusalem and told the two staff and seven children that they would have to leave immediately. A prayer vigil was held as the bulldozers moved in and knocked the building down. Staff say that they had been trying to get a building permit for some time but had been repeatedly refused.

The day after the building was knocked down, the Jerusalem Construction and Planning Committee granted planning permission for three new ultra-orthodox settlements in the Arab part of the city. According to a World Bank report, more than 80 percent of the illegal buildings in Jerusalem are in the Jewish, or western, half of the city. However, more than 80 percent of the demolition orders are served on buildings in the Arab half.

The outside world cannot claim that it doesn't know what is going on in East Jerusalem. In the summer of 2007, the International Committee of the Red Cross became the latest organisation to condemn Israel's colonisation of Arab areas. According to the ICRC, Israel is 'reshaping the development of the Jerusalem metropolitan area, with far-reaching humanitarian consequences'.

The Red Cross report, which was not meant to be made public but was leaked, said Israel was furthering 'its own interests or those of its own population, to the detriment of the population of the occupied territory'. The committee accused Israel of being 'in contravention of both the letter and the spirit of occupation law'.

The ICRC points out that Israel's construction of the wall around the city, the building of a ring of new settlements around the eastern sector, and the construction of new settler roads, on which the Arabs may not travel, is slicing up the Arab half of the city and cutting it off from the West Bank. The aim of these developments, says the committee, is 'to consolidate a greater Jerusalem': in other words, a greater Jewish Jerusalem.

There was nothing terribly new in what the Red Cross was saying; what is significant about this report is that the Red Cross is the world's watchdog on international law. Part of its role is to monitor breaches of the Geneva Convention and to try, albeit quietly, to get countries to meet their obligations under the convention.

But Israel does not accept that it has such obligations. Once the report was leaked, the Israeli government's response was that the whole basis of the report was flawed because Israel does not consider East Jerusalem to be 'occupied'. It was annexed. It is legally ours, say the Israelis, even if no one else agrees with us.

The relevant law, which is part of the Geneva Convention, forbids the occupying power from shifting its population into an occupied area in order deliberately to alter the demographic balance. The basis of the Israeli argument that East Jerusalem is not 'occupied' territory is that it was not sovereign territory when Israeli forces captured it in 1967. It had been under Jordanian control since 1948 and, before that, under British-mandate rule pending the division of Palestine into Arab and Israeli states.

'Israel violates international law with impunity', according to the then Palestinian information minister, Mustapha Barghouti, in an interview with the *International Herald Tribune* after the Red Cross report appeared in the *New York Times*. 'And it couldn't continue this blunt violation for forty years if it did not feel impunity towards the international community.'

According to an opinion poll published as recently as two years ago, almost half of Israelis agree with the idea of sharing the city of Jerusalem with the Arabs. An opinion poll carried out for the country's best-selling daily newspaper, *Yedioth Ahronoth*, suggested that 49 percent of Israelis agree with the idea of dividing up Jerusalem and ceding part of it to the Palestinians, in the framework of a peace deal. The poll indicates that half of Israelis would agree with handing Jerusalem's Arab areas back to the Palestinians, with the Jewish neighborhoods and the Western Wall, or Wailing Wall, remaining in Israeli hands.

This poll suggests that even in bad times, many Israelis are at least prepared to consider a compromise on one of the most controversial issues to be decided in final-status negotiations. If the talks on Jerusalem were to take place when all other issues had been agreed, perhaps the problem is not as intractable as many commentators believe.

Many secular Israelis would be quite happy to carve up the city, providing that this was part of a genuine peace deal. As long as the Jewish holy sites are in Israeli hands, then they would support the plan. Symbolism aside, many of them could not care less about the city, seeing it as a place now dominated by narrow-minded religious fanatics of all creeds, including their own. As a result, there has been a flight from the city by the secular majority in recent years.

But the peacemakers still have to contend with the fundamentalist attitudes of the ultra-orthodox community and the greed for land on the part of the ultra-nationalists. These two groups vehemently oppose the sharing of any areas of the city. When it comes to sharing those parts of the city that contain the Muslim and Judaic shrines, a carve-up seems virtually impossible, given the close proximity of these shrines.

I asked the former Chief Rabbi of Ireland, David Rosen, whether, from a strictly religious standpoint, it is possible to reach a compromise that would enable the two communities to share this small space. 'If people were reasonable, they would realise that the Almighty has been very generous to us in putting these various holy sites together,' he replies. 'Of course we can share them. In fact, that's the beauty of it.'

Some ultra-religious nationalists in Israel feel that it is a matter of religious pride to assert control of the northern part of the Temple Mount because it is the site of the holiest of holies. They would like to have some Jewish presence in the southern part. To the Muslims, this sounds as though their claim is being denied. Then there are the extremists who want to demolish the mosques and rebuild the Temple. From time to time, there have been various plots by fanatical Jews to blow up the Muslim section of the Mount, the Harram Al Sharif.

'There are those who take it to an extreme,' says Rabbi Rosen, 'and when they take it to an extreme, they become idolatrous. They take a means and they turn it into an end. Those elements are a minority, but a vociferous minority, and a very aggressive minority, and they can sometimes lead politicians by the nose,' he says, without naming any names.

But as far as you are concerned, there is no reason why the two faiths cannot coexist? 'In terms of the rabbinical establishment, in terms of the mainstream, there is absolutely no reason why Muslims can't have exclusive control over what is on top of Temple Mount and the Jews can't control what is below, which is the Western Wall.'

According to Rabbi Rosen, religious leadership should be 'a moderating force'. There should be a religious regimen in which there is cooperation and coordination. 'That's what some people on both sides have been trying to work on for the past number of years. But the problem is the political manipulation of religion.'

10

An Irishwoman in the Firing Line

Seventy-six-year-old Irishwoman Malka Meron is in the line of fire once again. Malka left Dublin more than fifty years ago to live in a land that was safe for Jews, and someone has been trying to kill her ever since. I have known Malka for nearly twenty years. We met when I was making a television documentary about Irish people living in Israel. Then I went back to see her as the first Gulf war started and Saddam Hussein was threatening to attack Israel with Scud missiles carrying chemical and perhaps biological warheads. This time it's the Islamic Jihad group firing rockets from Gaza towards her home in Kibbutz Zikim, just north of the strip.

Kibbutz Zikim, which is home to a couple of hundred people, was established on a few acres of dry land beside the coast, just south of the city of Ashkelon. Through extensive use of irrigation, they have created grassy areas all around, and small pathways lead through to the neat little detached bungalows, each with its own patch of garden front and back. There are tall trees and lots of shrubbery, and after the winter, when the meagre rains arrive, the brightly coloured flowers and plants will

141

bloom for a short time. Everything is neat but not overly groomed.

But it is the silence that really strikes you. There is little or no traffic. People leave their cars near the entrance and walk around the compound. Everything is close by. There is no rush, no pressure. Or so it appears.

'They hit us with rockets again this morning,' says Malka, pointing towards the banana plantation just outside the perimeter fence. The kibbutz has an early-warning system in place. There is a little intercom in each house which crackles into life every day or so, telling people to stay away from their windows. But it's more like a late-warning system, because they can't tell that rockets are on the way until the first one hits and they hear the bang. So they just get warning of the second missile. Or the third.

Maybe it is all the stress, but since I saw her last, Malka has had a stroke, and on the morning I arrive, doctors at the local hospital have removed two small growths from her face and left her with two bandages taped to her right cheek. 'I'm a bloody wreck,' she tells me in a Dublin accent as strong as the day she left Stamer Street more than half a century ago. 'I don't have the energy to get out of the way of a rocket even if I saw it coming.'

A few months ago, a rocket hit the kindergarten and several children were injured. All of them were terrified. Their parents banded together and raised some money to build a massive concrete cladding to erect around the kindergarten, and another for the building that houses the school for the older kids. An ugly cement frame, supported by ten-metre-high pillars – painted pale purple in an attempt to jolly it up – surrounds the vulnerable communal buildings. 'When I saw that happening,' says Malka, 'I really felt that we were under siege, and I was frightened. But you kind of get used to it.'

Like most Israelis, Malka believed that when Israel pulled its soldiers and illegal settlers out of Gaza in 2005, relative peace would be restored. 'We were being a bit idealistic,' she admits. 'We were hoping things would go back to the way they were. We even thought that maybe the Arabs would come back to work on the kibbutz.' But the rocket fire resumed, and there are now daily calls in Israel for the army to go back into Gaza and kill the Palestinians responsible. 'That's all nonsense,' says Malka. 'What can the army do against one man who runs out into a field, fires off a couple of rockets and then scarpers home? I have heard they're paying these people a couple of hundred dollars to go and fire the rockets. Some fellow is desperate to feed his family, so he is willing to do it. How can an army deal with that?'

There's an Irish connection with two of the big names in the early history of the Jewish state. Yitzhak Shamir was one of the Jewish resistance leaders who fought the British during their mandate over Palestine in the 1940s. Shamir, whom the British considered a terrorist, was greatly influenced by the guerrilla tactics of Michael Collins and attempted to emulate the Irish fighter. He even used the name 'Michael' as his *nom de guerre*. However, Shamir was less than impressed with Collins's decision to sign the treaty with Britain, and reportedly said that the Zionists should never settle for less than all of the country.

Both Shamir and another former 'terrorist', Menachim Begin, went on to become prime minister of Israel. Begin was the Israeli leader who gave then-defence minister Ariel Sharon the order to invade Lebanon in the early 1980s. Begin was to claim subsequently that he had been misled by Sharon about the scale of the Lebanon operation, and Sharon was demoted for his deceit. But while Sharon was to make a triumphant return to politics, Begin never recovered from the debacle of the Lebanon war, and ended his days as a recluse.

Menachim Begin was to be Malka Meron's inspiration for coming to Israel. In 1948, Begin came to Ireland because, as a wanted terrorist, he couldn't go to England, and he wanted to speak to some Zionist activists from there. When in Dublin, he spoke to a gathering from Ireland's small Jewish community.

Seventeen-year-old Muriel Brown was in the audience when Begin gave what she remembers as a thrilling speech about the Jews going back to their homeland after two thousand years. 'He talked about building a new society, creating a new Jew. I was terribly impressed,' she remembers.

Muriel become a Zionist, went off on summer camp to England, and eventually decided to quit Trinity College, where she had been studying languages. 'I remember the night I told my father I was leaving,' she says. 'It was on St Patrick's night in 1948. I waited up until eleven o'clock for him to come home, and then I told him about my plans. I remember him saying: "If you leave university, don't bother coming back, because I won't pay for you to go back to Trinity." I said: "Don't worry, I won't be coming back."'

After working with the Zionist youth movement for a few years in England, Malka decided to immigrate to the Jewish state and live the dream. Arriving in Israel in 1956 was something of a rude awakening for her. The land that the young pioneers were to work was more malarial swamp than milk and honey. They lived in tents and huts, and shared one tap; the toilet was a hole in the ground. 'I remember the Israelis, the ones born here, looked down on us Europeans. They thought we were soft and a little prim and proper. I remember it being difficult but enjoyable,' says Malka.

A few months after Malka arrived in Israel, the Suez crisis erupted. The Egyptian leader, General Abdel Nasser, nationalised the Suez Canal, and the Israelis, in collusion with the British and French, invaded Egypt to take control of the vital waterway. The Israeli 'adventure' ended when the Americans stepped in. 'It was a quick reminder that, even though we had a state, we were still involved in a fight for our existence,' she recalls.

By now, Malka was married to an Englishman called David. Their relationship lasted seven years. 'Too long,' she says with a laugh. 'I suppose I didn't really know him. We married in England and came over on the boat together. It was only when we got here that I got to know him.'

The land that Malka and the others settled was once known as Hirbia, and was an Arab farming community. This part of southern Israel, which borders the Gaza Strip, now has no Arab inhabitants. Much of the land around here was captured in 1948 by the Israeli army's Givati Brigade, under the command of a man called Yigal Allon, who relentlessly pursued a policy of ethnic cleansing. When the Zionists took over, a left-wing, secular kibbutz was established by a contingent of South Americans and some Europeans. They renamed it 'Zikim' (meaning 'Source of Light') and grew citrus fruits and vegetables. The patch of land where the kibbutz sits was once the property of a rich Arab landowner called Mussa Al Alami. As the Zionists began to arrive in Palestine in increasing numbers, the wily sheik read which way the winds of change were blowing and did a quick deal, selling the land to the Zionists before it was seized.

Al-Alami took the money, gathered his possessions and fled with his wives to Jordan, where he became a member of parliament. The Palestinian peasant farmers who had worked the land for a few shillings a week were scattered in all directions. All traces of where they once lived, along with the scores of other Arab villages in the area, were razed to the ground. Many of the Arabs who fled eventually ended up in the squalor of the refugee camps in Gaza. The sheik's old home, a large building of carved stone which once contained spacious courtyards and beautiful arched window frames, still stands on a hill in the southern corner of the kibbutz. From the flat roof of the now-dilapidated building, you can clearly see the crowded tower blocks of Gaza City, where many of the Arab families who fled from, or were driven out, of this area now live. That old stone house, and another smaller building, a hundred metres away, which housed the sheik's harem, are all that remains of the communities which used to live here.

Between the two world wars, and even after the first intifada, the kibbutzniks and the Palestinian people of Gaza maintained a kind of workable arrangement. Hundreds of Arabs made their way up from Gaza every day to pick fruit and vegetables in the area. They were day labourers earning a pittance for a long day's toil on what had been their own lands. They did it because they had nothing else.

It helped that the kibbutz members were always left wing and favoured some form of coexistence with the Arabs. Even in the last election, more than 70 percent of the members of the kibbutz voted for the left-wing Meretz Party, which supports a return by Israel to the pre-1967 borders. Not that such a move would make much difference to the Arabs from around Zikim: that settlement was established on lands captured in 1948, so any such deal would not allow for the people of Hirbia to get their lands back.

But the second intifada, and the virtual collapse of the kibbutz movement, put an end to all contact between the two communities. The Palestinians of Gaza are now completely fenced it and denied access to work in Israel. Meanwhile, the great socialist experiment of the kibbutz movement has essentially failed. The huge economic slump of the 1980s and 1990s meant that many kibbutzim had to shut down their fruit- and vegetable-growing businesses and sell off the land. Many diversified into more industrial projects, and the kibbutzniks were forced to commute into the towns and cities. Instead of being self-sustaining rural communities, as had been originally planned, the kibbutzim became just like all the other suburbs from where people commuted to work. These changes have brought about something of a revival in the kibbutzim's financial situation, but the old socialist ideals have been ditched, and on more than half of the country's three hundred kibbutzim, the idea of equal pay for everyone, regardless of the job they do, has been abandoned.

In the 1970s and 1980s, when Israel refused even to countenance the notion of a Palestinian state, and when meeting anyone from the Palestine Liberation Organisation was forbidden, Malka and the left-wing peace activists in Zikim continued to meet members of the PLO. Any Israeli engaging with the Arabs was viewed with great suspicion 'But we had to keep talking. We *still* have to keep talking,' Malka tells me. 'Even as recently as seven years ago, before the second intifada, a gang of us used to go down to Gaza for a night out. I remember going down to Gaza City to a great fish restaurant, and we had no trouble with anyone. But that's finished now, and we'll never get that back. It too far gone.'

Malka blames the former presence of Jewish settlers in Gaza for much of the souring of the relationship between Arabs and Israelis. 'Some of the religious settlers were really vicious,' she says. 'They treated the Arabs very badly.' Then there was the backlash. 'The husband of a friend of mine went down to Gaza one time and was beaten to death. For a lot of people around here, that coloured everything.'

The Gaza settlers have now been evacuated, but the presence of half a million settlers in the West Bank and East Jerusalem is still a major problem. 'Most Israelis living on this side of the 1967 "green line" would be happy to give back most of what's on the other side, but the settlers keep saying no,' says Malka. 'They can talk about entitlements as Jews wishing to live near Jewish holy sites in places like Hebron, but they can't demand the right to own these places. By doing that, they are bringing things to a ridiculous conclusion.' Malka points out that, in opinion poll after opinion poll, a clear majority of

Israelis support a deal on the basis of re-establishing the old 'green line', or the border drawn up after the 1948 war. But why, I ask her, do they then continue to vote for governments that either oppose that deal or purport to agree with it but do nothing to implement it?

'The people didn't vote for peace in the last two elections,' Malka explains. 'They voted for security; they voted for the strong arm. The people were not thinking about a political strategy. They went with what they thought was good for them, at least in the short term. It's not always pleasant for the people to hear the truth, to hear that they are not entitled to have what they want, so our politicians don't tell them.'

If the two sides ever get back to serious negotiations, Malka is sure that there will have to be some real compromises on both sides if any agreement is to work. Many of the settlements will have to go. The neighbouring Arab states will have to absorb hundreds of thousands of refugees, because they cannot return to their lands in what is now Israel. And Jerusalem? Who will control the Holy City? 'It has to be under international control,' Malka suggests. 'There is simply no way the two sides can agree to share it except under international control.'

'In my lifetime – which isn't very long – I can't see any change,' says Malka, managing to sound resigned rather than depressed. 'I am just glad that my grandchildren have finished their army service, because I can't see any sign of peace.' And can the two sides eventually make peace? 'They can. They can because they have to,' she insists. 'There is no other way. We cannot go on like this . . . but we have to fight towards it. And we have to fight to avoid being pessimistic. We have to do everything we can to help bring peace about, and we are not doing that now. Neither the Palestinians nor the Israelis. I can't do it any more. I am too old and too tired. It's up to the present generation now.'

11

'You Have to Help Us Get Out of Here!'

'You have to help us get out of here!' Mohammad was scream-ing down the phone trying to be heard above the rattle of gun-fire. It was the summer of 2007, and Hamas and Fatah gunmen were battling it out for control of Gaza. Mohammad, a Gaza businessman, was telling me that he was afraid that he and his family would be killed. Even during the worst of the fighting with the Israeli army over the previous six years, I had never heard him so frightened. 'We will try to go to Egypt,' he told me. 'After that I do not know what will happen, but I do not care. It could not be worse than here.'

Anybody who could get out of Gaza was getting out. Some said they hoped to come back. Others vowed never to return. Mohammad told me that he was thinking of boarding up his apartment, piling his wife and kids into the car, and heading for the border. 'It is crazy here,' he said. 'These people are crazy. They are shooting at everything. After this, there will be no peace in Gaza. Never.'

What happened in Gaza that summer didn't happen overnight. It had been festering for some time. But the descent into abject poverty, malnutrition, lawlessness, internecine fighting and downright despair was still shocking, given the relative optimism that had existed at the beginning of 2006. When the Israelis pulled their settlers and troops out of Gaza in August 2005, no one there believed that this meant an end to the occupation. They knew that Israelis troops were still in position just outside the locked gates. The Israeli air force remained in the skies above, and the Israeli navy controlled the waters around them. But the internal checkpoints were gone. The division of Gaza into three separate zones – which had prevented people from travelling freely, or from travelling at all, in this small stretch of land – had ended.

And the hated settlers had gone. The six thousand Jews, each of whom had occupied more land and used more fresh water than a dozen Palestinian families, had been packed up and moved out. The Arabs expressed delight at the sight of the settlers being dragged from their homes by Israeli soldiers and police. 'Now they know how we feel for forty years,' one old man in Gaza City told me afterwards. A Palestinian father of six children, interviewed before the disengagement began, told me how, when the settlers were gone, his kids would be able to get to the sandy beach near their home for the first time in their lives.

In early 2006, there was talk that the agricultural enterprises that had been built by the Israeli settlers would be taken over by a Palestinian co-operative funded by the World Bank. There was cautious optimism too that maybe the Palestinians could create some kind of holiday village somewhere along the beautiful long beaches of the Gaza Strip. 'We are thinking of calling it the "Gold Coast",' one businessman joked at the time. But the first priority had to be the clearing of the land where the settlers had lived to build new houses for the desperate families living in the worst of the overcrowded refugee camps.

The EU and the UN were engaged in negotiations with the Israelis to try to get the occupying power to allow the creation of a new port terminal just south of Gaza City. If there was progress on that front, the Israelis might even allow the Palestinians to reopen Gaza International Airport. The airport was shut down by the Israelis shortly after the intifada began. The security staff who still patrol the area showed me the bombed runway and the destroyed radar system, and gave me a tour of the dusty VIP lounge, which had once welcomed US president Bill Clinton and Taoiseach Bertie Ahern.

At the end of 2005, things in Gaza were not exactly good, but they were looking better. But then came the Palestinian elections of January 2006. When Hamas won these elections with a massive majority, most Palestinians believed that they had done what the outside world had asked, and held free and fair elections. The rewards would surely follow. But the international community was far from happy. The Americans, the EU and, naturally enough, Israel clamped a triple lock on the new administration. There would be no contacts, and no cash, until the Islamic party (1) recognised the State of Israel, (2) agreed to honour all previous agreements between the Palestinian Authority and Israel, and (3) ended the violence for good. Hamas was well and truly hobbled, and the people were about to pay the price.

After more than eighteen months of the boycott, my friend Mohammad Atief, a businessman in Gaza, was practically in tears as he served tea and described the situation. 'The people are very, very angry because of this boycott. How can you do this to us?' he asked. 'We knew we could expect no help from Israel, and not much from their friends the Americans. But

Europe? Europe was supposed to be helping us. Now you are punishing us, after we did what you asked us to do.'

For Mohammad and many like him, Europe is no longer to be trusted. 'We believed that Europe would help us, but you take the side of the Israelis and the Americans, and it is the Palestinians who have to do everything. Why doesn't Europe tell the Israelis to stop the violence? They came here after the soldier, Shalit, was kidnapped and killed four hundred people, many women and children, and nobody stopped them.'

Mohammad does not support either Hamas or Fatah. In the election, he voted for an independent candidate. But he thinks that Hamas should be given a chance to do something. 'At least allow them to try to create some order, so that we can get on with out lives,' he says. 'The peace process can wait. All we want to do now is eat.' Then he laughs because, as he says this, his wife Fatima brings out a tray of sandwiches. Mohammad's brother Rami is also with us. Rami owns a small grocery shop in the centre of Gaza City. I tell him that I will call in to see him there soon and buy something. 'Yes,' he says, 'please come if you want to buy some shelves, because that is all I have.'

Mohammad looks closely at the plate of sandwiches before picking up a piece of toasted pita bread. 'Here,' he says, offering me a sandwich, 'this one has cheese. I will eat the *zimzam*.' *Zimzam* is a kind of paste made from olive oil and herbs. It is what the family has been surviving on for more than a year.

Embarrassed to be offered what little real food the family has, I try to change the subject, and ask Mohammad how his two young children are. He has a boy and a girl, aged two and four, and another little one on the way. He tells me that his daughter Rheema has been to the hospital a couple of times suffering from severe stomach cramps. The doctors think that she has a parasite. An American doctor in Gaza once told me that she tested every child who came through her clinic for parasites, and more than 90 percent of the kids suffered from some form of this problem.

Mohammad's son Adnan has been having psychological problems, which are also common among the children in Gaza City. The last time I was in the apartment, the little boy was having nightmares and could not sleep.

'He is getting better now that the big bangs have stopped,' says Mohammad. The 'big bangs' are the sonic booms used by the Israelis to terrorise people. The blast is created by low-flying F-16 fighter jets, which swoop over the city and then bank sharply to create the boom. There is no warning, and the plane has already turned and is halfway back to Israel before the blast hits. The boom shakes entire buildings, and causes the roofs of some poorly constructed homes to collapse. The windows shake and sometimes shatter. Even the beds quake. For a few horrible seconds, you think it's a massive bomb, and your instincts tell you to dive for cover before debris flies in on top of you. For ten minutes afterwards, your nerves jangle.

To achieve maximum terror effect, the attacks usually came in the middle of the night or in the early morning. The birds go berserk, dogs howl, and you can hear the neighbours' children screaming. The sonic booms represent collective punishment of the worst kind.

After a spate of attacks in 2006, Mohammad's little boy could not sleep properly for weeks. He was wetting the bed every night. If he went to school at all, he just sat there, either crying or falling asleep, until the teacher eventually had to call his father and tell him to come and pick him up. A year later, he was only just recovering from the ordeal.

Mohammad brings the conversation back to the sanctions and the boycott imposed on the Palestinian areas by the West. 'What does the West think they will achieve by this boycott?' he asks. 'Do they think that we will rise up and overthrow Hamas?' I tell him that the stated intention of the boycott is to force Hamas to agree to the three basic principles outlined by the international community. 'So they do this by starving my children?' he asks. 'Look at him,' he says, pointing to Adnan, who is now sitting beside his father. 'Look at him. Does he look like a leader of Hamas to you?'

I ask the brothers if they think there is any possibility that Hamas will agree to the conditions. Rami speaks first. 'When will the West learn that the problem is not with the conditions? The problem is with the Israelis. The problem is with the occupation. If you end the occupation, then you will not need all these conditions. It's as simple as that.'

Mohammad tells me that he does not have a problem with recognising the State of Israel. 'What problem could I have?' he says. 'It is there; it is not going away. I will recognise it. But which Israel do you want me to recognise? Is it the one on the 1948 borders? The one that has 78 percent of the land? Because yes, I will recognise that one. But if you ask me to recognise the one that rules over the other 22 percent and rules over me, that I will not [do]. I would rather die first.'

'And what about the agreements?' interrupts Rami. 'When did the Israelis ever honour any agreement? Under the Oslo agreement, they were supposed to leave much of the land of the West Bank to the Palestinian Authority. Did they go? No, they did not go. They stayed and took more and more Palestinian land, and built more and more settlements.'

I ask if the disengagement – the pull-out of settlers and soldiers – has made any real difference to their lives. He says that it has, because there is greater freedom of movement inside the Strip. But he says that the disengagement has also made things worse,'because everybody on the outside thinks that the occupation has ended and that we should stop fighting. But the occupation has not ended.'

Before leaving, I ask Mohammad and Rami whether they support the firing of rockets into Israel from Gaza. I tell them about my Irish friend Malka, who lives in the firing line in Kibbutz Zikim. 'Ah yes, Zikim,' says Mohammad. 'I know Zikim. I know people from Zikim. They live now in Beach Camp in Gaza. They don't call it 'Zikim'. They have their own name for it from when it was an Arab village.' Does that mean that, in his view, it is a legitimate target? 'There is an Israeli army base beside it,' says Mohammad. 'Maybe they are trying to hit that, or maybe it's the power station in Ashquelon they are trying to hit,' he says. 'But if you're asking if [we think] it is OK to fire rockets at old women and children in a school, we do not. But do not expect us to do anything about it. You think I should go and ask Islamic Jihad to stop firing the rockets? I will go if you want me to go, but they will not stop. They will not stop until the occupation has ended. Tell your Jewish friend from Ireland that.' Then, as we move towards the door, his brother Rami leans down and picks up the last remaining sandwich from the plate and hands it to me. 'Here,' he says, laughing, 'give this to her. It is *zimzam*. Take this *zimzam* to Zikim and tell her that this is what we are eating here!'

On the way back into Gaza City, I pass the harbour. There are quite a few armed policemen around, but no sign of any fishermen. Normally the little fishermen's harbour is teeming with people at this time of day. The Israelis must have closed it again. About three thousand fishermen work out of this port. They used to make just enough to support their families. But now most of them are supporting as many as eight or ten families from the extended clan.

The Israeli patrols at sea continue. Since the withdrawal, six fishermen have been killed, and more than twenty injured. Scores have been arrested for fishing outside the 'restricted zone'. Under the Oslo agreement, the restricted zone is supposed to be twenty nautical miles, or more than thirty kilometres, but the Israelis impose a limit of less than half that. If they catch anyone outside the zone, they order them to stop their boats, strip naked and swim in the sometimes-freezing waters to the Israeli patrol vessel. The fishermen say that their nets and other equipment have been wilfully destroyed by the Israelis and that valuable generators have been confiscated.

This all adds to the general hardship and frustration experienced by the Palestinians. Nonetheless, despite the lack of funds, the Palestinian Authority was spending like crazy by taking on new staff. According to the World Bank, in 2006 the Authority added 1,300 people to the civil service and another 6,800 people to the payroll.

Even before Hamas came to power and the flow of funds began to dry up, the Palestinian Authority had an average monthly deficit of some €60 million – or about 60 percent more than its income. In 2007, its wage bill stood at €93 million a month. They were supposed to get this figure down to €80 million a month, but it was heading in the other direction instead. The last available figures showed that 165,000 people were working for the government, the civil service and the security forces combined. This is a rise of about 9 percent a year since 1999. The problem was that there was no money to pay them.

The World Bank says that the overall level of aid to the Palestinian Authority declined from $1 billion in 2005 to about $700 million in 2006. Since most development programmes in the Palestinian areas had been cut drastically, the bulk of this money was going on day-to-day spending. Part of the problem is accountability. Before the boycott of the Hamas administration came into force, the international community was trying to get all the foreign money to go through a single treasury account so that the donors could keep an eye on it.

The international community had to continue giving money to the Palestinians so as to avoid a collapse of the economy. As soon as Hamas took over the treasury, the West scrambled to find new ways to get the funds through to the people who needed it. The system is now so convoluted that it is almost impossible to monitor spending properly.

The local authority in Gaza City has been hardest hit. The municipality collects no more than 20 percent of its bills. The amount that the municipality is owed is already more than twice its annual budget. It is a similar situation in the West Bank. While thousands of young men are inducted into the security forces in order to do nothing all day except walk around with a gun and look tough, basic services like sewerage and garbage collection are being neglected.

When garbage is collected, there is nowhere safe to dump it, as the landfills are already stretched beyond their capacity. Hospital waste and other dangerous materials are being dumped alongside domestic rubbish. The consequences of this approach are already being felt. An EU report has warned that, because the entire Gaza Strip is built on coarse sand, which is extremely permeable, there is 'a permanent threat of contamination' of the water table.

The situation relating to the disposal of waste water is even worse. In early 2007, the waste-water treatment plant just outside Gaza City overflowed and swamped a nearby encampment, killing several people, including a number of young children. More than a year earlier, an EU report had warned that the situation at all of the treatment plants was 'critical'. But little or nothing was done. One of the other plants is so overloaded that thousands of cubic metres of raw waste water are being dumped directly into the sea every day.

One of the features of the Oslo Peace Accord, under which the Palestinian Authority was set up, was the creation of numerous branches of the security forces. At various times, there were between twelve and twenty of these branches in existence. The members of the security forces were all armed with weapons provided by the Israelis. The idea was that these forces would, apart from providing law and order in those areas which had been granted limited self-autonomy, prevent the various militant groups, such as Hamas, from carrying out attacks on Israel.

In the first few years after Oslo, Yasser Arafat ordered his forces to act against Hamas and Islamic Jihad. From time to time, they arrested hundreds of people and threw them in jail. On a number of occasions, there were fierce clashes between the two sides, resulting in dozens of deaths. While the Israelis always complained that the Palestinian Authority did not act often enough, most Palestinians felt that these arrests should not be being made at all. When the Israelis failed to meet their side of the Oslo bargain and hand over further territory to the Palestinians, the attempt to use Palestinian Authority security forces to end what most people saw as legitimate resistance became a real issue. Arafat became deeply unpopular in many quarters, especially in Gaza, where support for Hamas was strong. This was one of the primary causes of the infighting that plagued the Palestinians at the beginning of 2007 and almost led to civil war. The root causes of these clashes have not gone away, and they could erupt again at any time.

The Palestinian attitude towards the demands by Israel, and by the international community, including the EU, that the Palestinian Authority clamp down on those groups that are not on ceasefire was described by one PLO spokesman as 'the Israelis trying to subcontract the job of enforcing the occupation to the occupied'. Hamas will not accept this contract. They know that the cost of taking on this job will be a loss of credibility on the streets. Hamas spelled its position out clearly during the election campaign, saying that it viewed armed resistance as not only legitimate but essential.

Walid and Abdul joined Islamic Jihad on the same day. Walid was sixteen, Abdul was seventeen, and both were from the Jabalya refugee camp in Gaza City. Both men had lost family members in the fighting with the Israelis at the beginning of the current intifada. Walid had lost two brothers. His eldest brother was shot dead by an Israeli sniper during a curfew. His younger brother died when the car in which he was travelling was hit by a missile fired from an Apache helicopter. Walid says that his younger brother was involved with Islamic Jihad but that his older brother was not. Abdul, who also lost a brother, admits that his brother was a member of one of the militant groups but claims that he was not taking part in any operation the day he was shot by Israeli troops. 'They killed him because he was in the resistance, that is why,' he says.

We are talking in a house somewhere on the edge of Jabalya. A friend of the two young men picked me up in the city centre and told me to switch off my mobile phones. Together, we took a taxi to the refugee camp. After that, it was a five-minute walk through a warren of dirty little laneways. Where the passage widens, it is covered by netting or old blankets to provide cover from the sun and the long-range cameras mounted on the Israeli army balloon high above.

Outside the house, four armed men stand around smoking cigarettes. They watch, but say nothing, as I am shown inside. Walid is twenty now, and Abdul is twenty-one. They are both wearing paramilitary uniforms and holding automatic weapons. Behind them, on the wall, are a number of posters commemorating Islamic Jihad operations and the men who died in them. I begin by asking them if they have been firing rockets into Israel. 'We have carried out such operations,' says Abdul, 'and we will not stop until we have liberated all of the land of Palestine.'

Does that mean, I ask them, that Islamic Jihad would not accept a Palestinian state in the West Bank, Gaza and East Jerusalem, comprising 22 percent of the land? 'What is this 22 percent?' asks Abdul. 'There is only the Palestine [which is] occupied by the Jewish.'

I say that Hamas have said that it would accept a long-term truce if Israel withdrew from the land occupied after 1967. Would Islamic Jihad be prepared to do likewise? 'The Israelis will not leave those lands, so there will be no *hudna*, no cease-fire,' says Walid. 'The Israelis want to take all of our lands. This is why they are building the settlements in Al Quds [Jerusalem] and in the West Bank. Every day they take more and more land. They will not go. So we must continue the resistance and liberate all of the land.'

But what if they did end the settler programme and evacuate the settlers? Would Islamic Jihad consider a ceasefire then? 'The Israelis might agree to do this, but they will not leave,' Abdul replies. 'Many times they say they will leave this piece of land or that piece of land. But always they stay. And always they take more.'

I ask the two men what they hope to achieve by firing rockets at Israeli civilians. 'There are no civilians in Israel,' says Walid. 'They are all soldiers; they are all in the army.' The children are not in the army, I put it to him. 'They *will* be soldiers,' answers Walid. 'Every Israeli will be in the army, and they will come to Gaza and kill our children.'

'They must know [the pain and suffering we are experiencing],' says Abdul. 'We know the pain because of them. So let them feel the pain also. Then maybe they will stop.'

I tell the two men about Malka, the Irishwoman living in Kibbutz Zikim. I tell them that she is seventy-six and has never been in the army. I say that she and other Israelis support the idea of a Palestinian state in Gaza and the West Bank. Do they really want to kill people like that? 'Ah, the Israeli Left,' says Abdul, with a laugh. 'You mean like Shimon Peres, the one who makes the government with Sharon and then Olmert. Or the other one, Ben Elizier [the Labour Party Defence Minister], who was in the government when the Israelis came here and killed my brother. This is the one I should trust, maybe?'

'Let me tell you something,' he continues. 'The ones who say they are from the Left are the dangerous ones. We know what people like Sharon and Netanyahu want: they want to kill us. But the Left say they are our friends, and they still want to kill us.'

So what should I tell the Irishwoman? 'Tell her that we do not want to kill her. We want her to leave our lands and let us live in peace. Why doesn't she go back to Ireland? She should go back to her own country and give us our country,' Abdul says, and signals that the interview is over.

I tell them that she is probably not going anywhere, and neither are the rest of the six million Jews on the other side of the fence. 'Then there will be no peace,' Abdul says, shaking my hand, and calling for his friends to take me back to Gaza City.

12

LIVING UNDER OCCUPATION

Rheema, a Palestinian mother, is trying to take her three young children to see their granny in Nablus. It's a rainy morning in Ramallah, and Rheema is jostling with dozens of others trying to get a taxi at the crowded *minara*, the square, in the centre of Ramallah. The three kids are all under eight, and she is already having to cope with the first infant intifada of the journey as she tries to stuff the three of them into the back seat of a battered *sheroot*, or shared taxi. Two old women with covered faces are already in position, and are showing no willingness to share with the three noisy kids.

'I used to visit my mother once a week,' Rheema tells me as she struggled with youngest of her children. 'Now I can really only do this maybe one time every four weeks.' If the roads were free, the journey could be made in less than an hour; with all the checkpoints, it will take the whole day.

This is only the first of several taxis that Rheema must take. She will travel in this car as far as the first checkpoint, where she will have to prise the kids out, stand in line at an Israeli security checkpoint for anything up to three hours, get another taxi on the other side, and then continue until the next checkpoint. And the next. She has no way of knowing how many checkpoints lie ahead, or how long the journey will take.

'Will today be an easy day?' I ask her. 'There is no easy day,' she says. '*Inshallah*, I will have a good day. A good day is when I can get to Nablus. A bad day is when they turn me back. Sometimes when I am at the last checkpoint, they say no.'

Israel says that this system of checkpoints is necessary for security reasons and that the measures would not be necessary if the violence stopped. But even during lengthy ceasefires, the checkpoints stay in place, and there are frequent 'closures', when virtually nothing moves.

In the spring of 2007, the Israeli newspaper *Ha'aretz* collated all the data that is available about restrictions on movement imposed on the Palestinian population. The paper did its own research and also drew on information provided by the Israeli human-rights group Machshom, or Checkpoint Watch, and OCHA, the United Nations Office for the Coordination of Humanitarian Affairs in the occupied territories.

If you want an idea of what life is like living under occupation, here are some of the rules you have to obey. If you are from the Gaza Strip, you are not allowed to stay in the West Bank. If you are a Palestinian from the West Bank or Gaza, you cannot go into East Jerusalem. If you are from the West Bank, you can't go to Gaza. You are not allowed to enter the Jordan Valley. If you are not from any of the Palestinian villages or towns in the 10 percent of the West Bank caught between the Wall and the Green Line, you can't go there either. You can't go anywhere near any of the settlements. You can't go to some of the Palestinian villages near the settlements unless you live in one of them. You can't take your car into Nablus. You cannot travel abroad using Tel Aviv Airport. Even if you have a permit, you cannot use the land crossings used by Israelis or tourists. Residents of Gaza are not allowed to live in the West Bank.

Those are just some of the standing prohibitions. There are other rules that are applied periodically and can be introduced without warning and without a stated duration. They include banning residents of certain parts of the West Bank from travelling to the other areas of the territory. If you are aged between sixteen and forty and live in a city such as Nablus or Jenin, you are not allowed to leave that area at all. And you cannot take your car through the checkpoints that separate the upper and lower halves of the West Bank.

Then there is the whole system of travel 'permits'. There are too many types to list, but a typical one is the paperwork needed for someone from the West Bank to travel for medical treatment in Israel or in a Palestinian hospital in the Israeli-annexed East Jerusalem. First, you need a letter of invitation from the hospital. Then, a copy of all your medical reports. And you must be able to prove that the treatment you are seeking cannot be provided by a hospital in the West Bank. All of this could take weeks or months. Even when you get the permit, there is no guarantee that it will be honoured by the soldiers at a particular checkpoint on a particular day. Most people trying to get this sort of treatment are seriously ill. By the time they have gone through all the red tape to get a permit and an appointment and are actually in a position to make the journey, they could be dead.

In November 2005, an agreement on movement and access was signed by the Israelis and the Palestinian Authority, whereby checkpoints would be removed altogether, or conditions at the roadblocks improved, to make it easier and faster for the Palestinians to go about their daily business. In March 2007, OCHA drew up figures showing that there are a total of 546 checkpoints, roadblocks and gates. This figure represents a 44 percent increase on the number that existed in November 2005.

The majority of the checkpoints are located not between

the West Bank and Israel, but inside the West Bank, severing links between Palestinian areas. To the Palestinians, this is evidence that security is not the prime consideration. Some of the roadblocks can be justified on the basis of security for the West Bank settlements, but if the settlements are themselves illegal under international law, there can be no legal basis for imposing repressive restrictions on the movements of the Palestinians.

According to a recent World Bank report on freedom of movement, Palestinians are prevented from accessing some forty-one segments of highways in the West Bank. In other words, they cannot use about seven hundred kilometres of road. To the Palestinians, the barriers are there primarily to strangle their community. They see these mechanisms, like so many other measures that are used to enforce the occupation, as being designed to stifle the economy, subjugate the Palestinian population and generally add to their humiliation.

According to Shawan Jabarin of the Palestinian human-rights group Al Haq, the restrictions are all about Israel trying to beat them down and force them to submit to the occupation. As he sees it, the Israelis are trying to make life so unbearable for the Palestinians that, eventually, they will agree to forego independence in return for some semblance of a normal life. 'This is not a classic colonial regime in which the occupying power benefits from the natural resources of the area and has no intention of transferring the population out of the occupied zone,' he says. 'In this instance, Israel has targeted the land, and their aim is to push the people out so as to minimise the numbers of Palestinians living there.' The evidence for this, he claims, is the policy of the demolition of thousands of Palestinian homes, the uprooting of crops and fruit trees, the building of the Wall, and the imposition of restrictions on internal movements without real security needs.

165

A recent World Bank report found that Israel is preventing any possibility of the Palestinian economy being able to grow. The World Bank says that the restrictions on the freedom of movement, which prevent Palestinians from accessing some 50 percent of the West Bank, damages any prospects that the economy has of emerging from its current crisis. The report says that freedom of movement is now the 'exception rather than the norm' and that the series of policies and regulations, and the physical barriers, which are now in place are breaking the territory up into ever-smaller and more-disconnected cantons. From an economic point of view, these little enclaves cannot survive in isolation. Without easy access between them, they will simply wither and die.

It is not just the Israeli restrictions on movement that are stifling the Palestinian economy. The Israelis have almost complete control over anyone who is trying to run a business in the occupied territories. And they don't make things easy for these people.

Khalil and Salah are cousins who run a couple of firms selling household products from Ramallah on the West Bank. 'The amount of taxes, tariffs and levies we pay to the Israelis for the privilege of doing business means that a lot of money is simply going out of the economy forever,' says Khalil. 'All that cash that comes in from the World Bank, the NGOs and the EU is not circulating here. It is being sucked out to Israel by this tornado.' More than a few times, the men have thought about simply selling up and leaving. But for now, they will stay. 'We have an investment. We cannot just up and leave, because no one will buy our business,' says Salah. 'Besides, this is our home; my great-grandfather started this business. We want to make it work. If people like us left, the place could collapse into chaos. This could be a Third World country in just six months.'

Khalil admits that he has already sent his wife and kids out of the country. 'I have to give my family some chance,' he says, 'but I will hang on here as long as I can.' Both men say that their cash reserves are long gone; another long curfew could finish them off altogether. They count themselves lucky because they have some personal savings. 'Our employees have nothing,' says Salah. 'There is no social welfare here if things go wrong. On what we can pay them, they can feed their families chicken twice a month and meat maybe once a month. There is no such thing as going out. And if you get sick, you have to borrow money.'

Khalil and Salah tell me that the first problem they have when it comes to running their business is getting raw materials in. Everything has to be bought from Israel, and they pay about 15 percent more than Israeli firms do. Trying to import directly from a third country is even more expensive. Once they get the stuff in, it still has to get through the checkpoints. Khalil says he is lucky if he gets one shipment in three through on time. 'We have to use jeeps to carry materials over the hills and back roads,' says Salah, 'because the good roads are open only to settlers; they are closed to us.'

Israeli suppliers, on the other hand, find it very easy to get their goods in to the Palestinian areas. They have to deal with much less security, so they frequently dump their extra stock on the Palestinian market at below what it costs to produce such products locally. At the same time, the Palestinian companies cannot compete on the Israeli market. 'It is very, very difficult,' says Khalil. 'You can't import raw materials, manufacture something, and then resell to Israel. If you want to import, you have to sign a paper saying that you will not re-export to Israel. That's about protectionism.'

Besides, if Palestinian companies want to trade with Israel, they have to have an Israeli partner. Because of this, there has been an 80 percent drop in the number of textile companies operating in the Palestinian territories. Because they rely so heavily on trade with Israel, most of them have moved to Jordan, because of the freedom of movement there. They can ship their goods from Amman to Tel Aviv directly.

There is a similar squeeze on the agriculture business. The

Palestinians used to have a trade with Jordan in fruits and vegetables that was worth millions. Now that has been blocked because they cannot transport the goods directly to Amman; they have to go through Israel. Khalil says that if he wants to export his goods into the wider Arab market, say to Kuwait, then they still have to go through Jordan. 'That means that we pay about treble what it costs a Jordanian to sell to Kuwait. This is about nothing else but blocking our trade,' he claims. 'It's about killing us off.'

On top of this, strict quotas are imposed on the Palestinians regarding what they can produce themselves. 'Even the number of cows we can have here is limited,' says Khalil. 'That means that we have to import thousands of litres of Israeli milk every day.' Salah says that this quota system frightens off any potential investors from outside. 'Who is going to put money into a factory here if they are being told how much they can make?' he asks.

The election of Hamas in 2006 has led to new restrictions on Palestinian trade. 'Say I want to export to Ireland,' says Khalil, 'how will my customers pay me? Every kind of wire transaction is now closely monitored. You want to send me money from Ireland. The paperwork goes to New York to be cleared, and then sent to here. There is no direct wiring of money. If someone sends me a cheque, it could be six months before I get it.'

'We used to have an online security company in the United States,' says Salah. 'Suddenly they said: "Sorry, we cannot renew your contract because your government is Hamas."' They had the same problem with a company in South Africa. 'They told me, sorry, they can't do business because their parent company in the United States told them not to.'

Khalil and Salah say that they have had to lay off hundreds of workers over the past few years. So have most other big Palestinian companies. The smaller firms have simply closed down. The effects of the squeeze are being felt everywhere. At the local university, Beit Zeit, students come to school every day hungry. They can't concentrate. The standard of exam results is dropping. To combat this, the college has asked businessmen like Khalil and Salah to sponsor a student for $30 a month so that he or she can buy one meal a day at the college cafeteria. 'I can't afford $30 a month any more,' says Khalil, 'so I gave them two years' supplies of detergents free. That's all I could do.'

I question the rationale behind all of this. Why would it be in the interests of the Israelis to squeeze the Palestinian economy so tightly that it collapses? Would the descent into chaos that would ensue not merely enflame the situation? 'Firstly, they are making a lot of money out of us, and that keeps the Israeli business community happy,' says Salah. 'But there is also a political objective. The Israeli policy used to be about trading land for peace. Now the deal is going to be trading peace for peace. They keep the land, and we get peace in return. They want the economic situation in the West Bank to be as bad as [it is in] Gaza. They want us to be so low, so desperate, that we accept anything. They have begun to imprison our minds.'

Most of the Palestinian labourers put their heads down and refused to look up when we arrived to film the building work at the Wall. A few of them did meet my gaze, their expressions a mixture of shame and deep resentment. These men were being employed to help erect the wall and security fence the Israelis were putting up around the West Bank. But the wall and fence were being built on land that had been confiscated from the Palestinians. It was their own countrymen who would suffer. The barrier they were erecting would separate tens of thousands of Palestinians from the surrounding areas and lock them into the newly created Bantustans.

169

The men were building a section of the Wall near the northern city of Qualqilya. They told me that they were from the south and were being bussed up every day to do the work. When the work in the north was completed, the huge construction teams would move down along the West Bank, and any Palestinian labourers from the north who wanted a job could get one. According to the United Nations, almost half the people in the West Bank are earning less than $2 a day. That will buy you a packet of cigarettes in Nablus.

After the Oslo agreements were signed, the Israelis began reducing the number of Palestinian day labourers who were allowed into Israel to work. After the outbreak of the intifada, that process was speeded up, and hundreds of thousands of workers were brought in to Israel from the Far East to replace the Arabs. But they still use Palestinian labour in some of the so-called industrial zones of the illegal settlements in the West Bank.

For the would-be Israeli producer, the start-up costs for new businesses in the settlements are considerably lower than in Israel itself. For one thing, the land is cheap because it has been provided by the government which took it from the Palestinians. Then, for every dollar invested in the start-up, the settler company receives a dollar from the government. Some of these companies abuse that system by getting false invoices showing inflated prices for the building of factory premises. The construction firms are owned by the Russian mafia, who then collapse the companies and disappear before anyone can question their costs. They even use cheap Palestinian labour to do the building work.

Some of the workers have permits; these permits are very difficult to obtain, because the employee has to be screened by the Israeli security service. This takes time, and the employers have to pay about €200 for each permit that is granted. Sometimes they don't bother getting permits and simply hire people illegally. People working like that are paid about eleven shekels an hour for a nine-hour day, in a six-day week. That is less than €2 an hour, and about 50 percent less than the legal minimum wage in Israel. But for the Palestinians, €2 an hour is big money, and they will do anything to keep those jobs. And they often do.

The workers say they are harshly punished if they turn up late, including being sent home for a week. If they give trouble or are sick, they can lose their jobs altogether. Employers don't have to worry about finding a replacement. And the cheap and ready supply of labour is only one of the reasons why Israeli firms locate in the settlements: they also receive tax breaks and can operate dirty industries that are not allowed in most parts of Israel. It's the same thing if there is an industrial accident. If a Palestinian loses a couple of fingers in a machine, he is simply sent home. There is no fear of a lawsuit. Israel's health and safety inspectors will not be calling around because an Arab worker was injured.

On the West Bank itself, those people who still have jobs have become migrant workers in their own country. To avoid the daily hassle of getting past the checkpoints to work in the cities, people have resorted to sleeping on the living-room floors of relatives or renting cheap accommodation. They will live like that for six days of the week and then go home at the weekend.

The checkpoints mean that they frequently either cannot get to work at all or arrive several hours late. And it is not just the delays that prompt the Palestinians to try to avoid the checkpoints: it is the humiliation and abuse they get as they try to go about their daily lives. Very often, they have to stand in the rain or in blazing sunshine for several hours to have their identity cards checked by Israeli soldiers.

At some of the busier checkpoints, there are frequent clash-es between Palestinians and Israeli soldiers. Sometimes, when hundreds of people are trapped on one side or the other in a queue that is going nowhere fast, trouble will start. First there is the usual jostling and pushing among the tightly packed crowd. Before long, a great heaving mass of people will start to career towards the checkpoint. The Israeli soldiers will fire tear gas and stun grenades into the crowd. Not beside them. Right into them. If some Palestinian youths respond by throwing stones at the Israelis, troops will open fire with live ammuni-tion. Sometimes they aim over the heads of the teenagers. Sometimes they aim lower.

Avi is an Israeli soldier who joined the refusenik movement Yesh Guvul in around 2002. Yesh Guvul, which means 'there is a limit', were a bunch of young conscripts and reservists who were refusing to serve in the occupied territories. They said that they were prepared to fight a war to protect their country but that they were simply not willing to enforce a military occupa-tion. When the group was formed, they were so concerned about being seen to be disloyal to Israel that they declined to be interviewed by the foreign media. Eventually they relented, and Avi, a combat veteran, told me something about his duties on the checkpoints.

He described how, when trouble broke out and the soldiers were being attacked by stone-throwers, he was instructed to open fire with live ammunition. This was an order from his unit commander, he said, and not something that was then in the army rule book. The army's fear is that, if a group of teenagers begins firing stones, a gunman would use the crowd as cover to approach the soldiers' position.

So they were told to shoot one of the youths to frighten them off and clear the area. Avi said that they were told simply to pick one and shoot him. I asked whether this was an order to shoot to kill, or just to injure. He told me that a teenager running quickly towards the checkpoint was not a target on which you can pick your shot. So the result was very often the same: the kid died.

Much of the time, Avi felt that his job was just to make life as difficult as possible for the Palestinians. He felt that many of his colleagues went along with this because if the Palestinians avoided the checkpoints, it made life easier for the soldiers. According to Israeli journalist Amira Hass, that policy is still in place at some checkpoints. She has reported how Palestinian farmers attempting to take their agricultural produce through checkpoints were being told that this was 'illegal' and were forced to make detours of about thirty kilometres to get their goods to the markets. She found that when the orders were repeatedly challenged, the soldiers came up with all sorts of spurious excuses to stop or delay the farmers from getting through. Sometimes it was an alleged 'security warning'; at other times, they told the farmers that there was construction work going on at the checkpoint.

While waiting to pass through a checkpoint one day, I watched as two Israeli soldiers, one male and one female, both in their early twenties, stepped out from behind the sandbags. The man was carrying a weapon that fires stun grenades and was obviously explaining to the woman how it worked. They stopped on the brow of a little hill below which scores of Palestinians were getting their minibuses and taxis. The young soldier took aim and fired a stun grenade right into the middle of the crowd. Women dropped shopping bags, grabbed their children and scattered. Men took cover behind cars. For a few minutes, there was panic. The two Israeli soldiers watched and laughed, and then calmly walked backed to their positions. Lesson over. That's how to terrify a civilian population.

I asked Avi, the former soldier, about the impact of actions like that. Did he not think that they were inviting the Palestinians to hate them? He did, and he told me that he had even said this to his commanding officer. The reply was that the Palestinians hated them anyway, so they might as well teach them who was in charge. This is easier for the Israeli soldiers to do if the Palestinians have been demonised or dehumanised.

13

'THIS IS A BATTLE FROM A DIFFERENT AGE'

What is it that the Israelis want? Sure, they want to live in peace in a Jewish state. That's the easy bit. But what do they want the Palestinians to have? Sadly, they haven't really reached a collective decision on the matter. The majority seem to want a Palestinian state, but there are very different views of how much land a future Palestinian state should cover, and how much power it should have. Only a tiny minority say that Israel should simply hand over all the lands that were seized in 1967 and be done with it. The vast bulk of Israelis want to keep much of East Jerusalem and the main settlements on the edge of the West Bank, and believe that the Palestinians refugees who lost their land should not be allowed to return to it. On top of that, they want any deal to impose strict conditions on the Palestinians, with statehood being granted in incremental stages. As a reward for good behaviour, the Palestinians will gradually be allowed to take on more responsibility for their own affairs.

But as many as a third of Israelis can be categorised as right-wing or extremely right-wing. The Right maintains that the Jewish state should give up nothing for the foreseeable future. The extreme Right argues that Israel should give nothing to the Palestinians: not now, not in the near future, not ever. In fact, the extremists argue that the Palestinians are not a race at all and that there should never be a Palestinian state, because its very existence would threaten the Jewish state. But if there is a clear divide between the various political parties, it is much harder to separate the views of the people who vote for them. The hard Left and the hard Right may be consistent in their voting habits, but the single biggest grouping, the so-called 'middle ground', swings left or right depending on what has been happening and what leaders are on offer. Right now, that majority has shifted to the right, or even the extreme right.

Traditionally, most of the Irish-born Jews living in Israel have been supporters of the left-wing Labour Party or the right-wing grouping of Likud. In this, they are a microcosm of the electorate as a whole. Since the 1970s, the two big parties, or a combination of the two, have controlled the political landscape in Israel. Since the outbreak of the current intifada, the two parties have been in broad agreement on the key issue of security. The Labour Party, badly bruised after their peace initiative collapsed in 2000, felt that they could only regain some credibility by supporting the militaristic adventures of Ariel Sharon and the Likud Party, which had defeated them in a series of elections.

In the last election, supporters of both Likud and Labour shifted across to the so-called 'centrist' Kadima Party, set up by Ariel Sharon and Ehud Olmert. But a series of blunders by Olmert over the Lebanon war of 2006 has prompted people from either camp to declare themselves disenchanted enough to revert to their original allegiances. In a sense, however, this is only because they have nowhere else to go. Many Israelis are now reluctant to place any real faith in either of the two main parties. It is a time of political indecision and confusion. People think that they know what they want; they just don't know who can deliver it.

Like all good barmen, Robert Segal refuses the offer of a pint before starting work. Segal is sitting in Molly Bloom's in Tel Aviv's Hayarkon Street, one of the several Irish bars he co-owns in the city, about to face into a twelve-hour shift. 'Where do you think you are? Dublin?' he says. 'It's only four o'clock in the afternoon. Come back at four in the morning, when we're closing, and buy me one.'

Forty-eight-year-old Robert left Terenure in Dublin in 1980. For a few years after leaving school, he worked for his father in the family's metal-works factory in Dublin's Wood Street, behind the Adelaide Hospital, turning out tableware and GAA medals, and lapel badges for the Blood Transfusion Service. He says he was 'a bit of a Zionist' back in the 1980s but admits that what really prompted him to emigrate to Israel was the sense that if he didn't get out of Ireland then, he would have stayed working in the family business for the rest of his life.

His first years in Israel were spent on a kibbutz, picking fruit, learning Hebrew and 'trying to become an Israeli'. He decided that the best way to do this was to volunteer for the army. This was 1982, just as Ariel Sharon was leading the Israeli army into Lebanon. 'Lousy timing' is how Robert describes it. Sharon, as defence minister, had told his prime minister, Menachim Begin, that 'Operation Peace for Galilee', as it was called, would involve an incursion of no more than forty kilometres into Lebanon to root out PLO fighters who were attacking northern Israel. In the end, Sharon led the Israeli troops all the way to Beirut – and created calamity for all involved.

In the beginning, the main fighting was between the Israelis and the PLO, who had been using south Lebanon as a base from which to attack Israel. But it was not long before Muslims, Christian and Druze (an offshoot of Islam) were all involved. Robert soon realised what he had got himself into. On an approach road to Beirut, his unit was passed by a jeep carrying a group of Christian Phalanges fighters. Moments later, the Christians suffered a direct hit from Druze fighters in the hills above. 'As we approached their burning jeep, I could not see anybody, so I presumed they got clear,' he remembers. 'But as we got up close, I saw the four burned-out bodies in the vehicle and thought, fuck, that could have been us.'

Corporal Segal and his colleagues had only discovered that they were sliding into the quagmire of a long war when they were ordered to prepare for an advance into Beirut. It was the first he had heard of going to the Lebanese capital. It was the first the Israeli public, or even the government, had heard of it too. Defence Minister Sharon had lied to everybody. As the Israeli army pushed further north, Sharon attempted to justify the advance as crucial to destroying the PLO forces. Back home in Tel Aviv, the protests against the war had already started, but the soldiers were oblivious to them. 'You are too busy trying to stay alive,' says Robert. Afterwards it hit home. 'We should have driven the PLO from the south and then gone home. Instead, we got sucked into Israel's Vietnam.'

Going into Lebanon, Robert believed that the Israelis were the good guys. 'I believed everything Israel did was right; the Palestinians were in the wrong. I believed it all.' But after his tour of duty in Lebanon, and a few spells in the West Bank, Robert began to change his opinion. 'In the West Bank, I began to think of Northern Ireland, and the whole situation with the Palestinians did not sit well with me at all,' he says. 'I didn't like what I saw. I began to see it wasn't all bravery and valour as the little nation defends itself. I didn't buy that any more. We were turning into the local bully.'

Robert became 'very left-wing', as he put it, for a time but, like many Israelis, those left-wing beliefs took a battering when the second intifada began in 2000. 'The suicide bombings shook me,' he admits. 'When I was in Ireland, I could see the reasons behind the bombings to some extent, but here, this deliberate targeting of innocent civilians, this blowing themselves up, I just could not forgive that.'

But the Israeli army kills innocent civilians too, I remind him. Lots of them. 'Sure they do,' he accepts, 'but we do not target civilians. We do not set out to kill non-combatants. I have served in the West Bank on many occasions, and I can honestly say that I have never seen an Israeli soldier deliberately kill a Palestinian civilian.'

But does this high figure of civilian casualties not cause him some discomfort, to say the least? 'Accidents do happen,' he accepts. 'I know soldiers who have killed innocent people by accident, in many different kinds of circumstances. They regret that. They have to go home to their families and try to live with what they have done. And a lot of them can't. Many of them still can't sleep at night because of what they did. But it was not deliberate. On the other hand, you have to accept that there is no such thing as a good occupation or a good army of occupation. It does not exist.'

If and when the two sides ever get to the negotiating table, Robert is clear where he stands on the key issues. He believes that the main settlement blocs in the West Bank will probably have to stay because they are large towns by now, but that Israel will have to give the Palestinians land of equal value in return.

And the smaller settlements deep inside the West Bank? 'They will all have to go,' he says. 'I had to guard these places when I was in the army, and I always asked myself: what am I doing here protecting a bunch of loons who don't even like me? I don't care much for settlers,' he continues, and then jokes: 'My solution has always been to give all of the West Bank back to the Palestinians on condition that they take the settlers too!'

Does he see any clamour from the Israeli side to begin negotiations? 'Not from the public. The suicide-bombing campaign has silenced the Left,' he says, 'and the majority – those in the middle, those who can swing right or left – are apathetic. People are saying that now that we have the Wall, the bombings have slowed, so we are back to normal, so it's wonderful. But it's not back to normal. The Wall works to some extent, but it won't solve the real problem. In the meantime, we have this false sense of security because nothing has really changed.'

Robert feels that it would take a very strong Israeli leader to push through any peace deal, because of the upheaval that any compromise might involve for Israeli society as a whole. 'Much as I disliked him, Ariel Sharon was probably one of the few political leaders with the strength to make something happen,' he says.

Now there is the added complication of the split between Hamas and Fatah, and the creation, in effect, of two Palestinian Authorities: one in Gaza and another in the West Bank. 'Even if they succeed in propping up Mahmoud Abbas in the West Bank, it still leaves us with the problem of Hamas in Gaza,' says Robert. 'The danger now is that if we continue to ignore Hamas and Gaza, then the area will become even more radical.'

Robert thinks that, in the end, Israel will simply have to deal with Hamas and that, in order to do that, they will have to engage with the Islamic group rather than maintain their current policy of isolation. But he concedes that the chances of that happening are not good.

So is he pessimistic about the prospect of peace in the near future? 'In five years, definitely not,' he says. 'In ten years, I would be sceptical. And in twenty years? Ask me again then!' If the conflict goes on much longer, does it become insoluble? 'Yes and no. Yes, in the sense that people can get more dug in.

No, in the sense that the world has moved on and is moving on quickly. This is a battle from a different age, and eventually the world is going to get tired of dealing with us and say, look, sort this out or you are on you own.'

Robert thinks that the consequences of the conflict, in terms of the damage that has been done to Israel, has been enormous. 'This has made Israeli society very violent and aggressive,' he says. 'It has caused huge poverty. There is a massive amount of potential being wasted. And it has turned people off religion. I have a lot of friends now who associate religion with the conflict, and they have turned away [from their religion]. They don't consider themselves primarily as Jewish any more; they think of themselves as Israeli. It's all very sad.'

Another Dublin-born Jew, Guy Gordon, voted for Kadima in the last election. Now he regrets it. Like Robert Segal, Guy feels that his adopted country is somewhat rudderless. He feels that the Palestinian question has become so vexed that he has begun to stop thinking about it. For him, a far more important issue now is the rampant corruption in the Israeli political establishment. 'This is a bit of a banana republic, really,' says Guy. 'There is this deep institutionalised corruption at many levels of government and public life.'

But he accepts that, sooner or later, the Palestinian issue will have to be faced and difficult decisions will have to be made. 'The occupation bothers me on a moral level,' he says. 'And it bothers me because of the huge damage it does to Israel's image in the rest of the world.' But like the majority in Israel, he lays much of the blame for the current impasse at the door of the Palestinians. 'I believe that the majority of them just want to live in peace and quiet,' he says, 'but there is an increasing number of them who have become brainwashed and self-delusional, and there is certainly no partner for peace among the Arab leadership.'

He thinks that many of the current problems stem from the education system in the Palestinian territories. 'It's not anti-Zionism, its anti-Semitic hate,' he says. 'Education is the poisoned well of Palestinian society. Biased textbooks and television [are] sending out messages of anti-Semitic propaganda, and because of that I don't think we are going to see real peace. Not in my generation, anyway.'

I put it to him that this hatred may have as much to do with the fact that Palestinian teenagers see their friends being killed, soldiers humiliating their parents at checkpoints, and heavily armed settlers destroying their crops and getting away with it as with the way in which the history of the Middle East is taught in Palestinian schools. Isn't it these things which really shape their view of Israel? He admits that this is 'partly true' and notes that many of the Israeli army's so-called security measures are 'ineffective' in terms of providing security and 'counter-productive' in terms of winning public trust.

The settlements are a major problem for Israel, in Guy's opinion. 'I have never figured out how the settlers have such a powerful hold over the corridors of power,' he says. 'There is a total lack of political will to deal with this issue, and among the public there is a tremendous amount of apathy.' He resents the fact that ordinary Israelis have to pay the price for the lack of leadership on this issue. 'Reserve soldiers like me have to go out there and risk our lives to defend them [the settlers],' he complains.

At the time of the Gaza disengagement, he supported the move, but now he thinks it was a mistake. 'All my right-wing friends warned that Gaza was going to be a base of terror, and they have been proved to be right,' he says. He accepts that Israel has not pulled out completely in the sense that it has not relinquished control over air and sea corridors around Palestinian areas, but he says that doing so would make the threat to Israel's security even greater.

On the question of security, he welcomes the construction of the so-called security barrier in the West Bank. 'The Wall has done its job,' he argues. 'There has been a drastic reduction in the number of suicide bombings because of it. It's not because of a sudden enlightenment on the part of the Palestinians.' But could the same result not have been achieved by building on the Green Line, instead of several kilometres east of it? 'Sure,' he admits.

When it comes to the issues of refugees, Guy is adamant that there can be no mass return of Palestinians who fled or were driven from their lands and homes in 1948. 'There is absolutely no precedent in history for such a thing,' he says.

And what about the Zionist dream? Has the Jewish state been realised in the full sense, and does it live up to his expectations? 'In terms of social structures, we still have much to do. The gap between rich and poor is far too wide; there is a high level of crime; there is corruption in government.'

But what is his feeling on the question of whether Israel is a place that is safe for Jews? 'It's not safe, but it is a place in which we can defend ourselves, and that makes us feel safer than anywhere else. Our own country will never turn on us the way others might do. You only have to look at how safe Jews felt in Germany in the 1920s and early 1930s to understand how this feeling comes about. Then, we had reached the upper echelons of German society, and we felt accepted and safe, yet just ten years later we were in the cattle trucks bound for the concentration camps.'

But in the twenty-first century, is the idea of a Jewish state, a state based on a religion, any religion, not something of an anachronism? 'Absolutely not,' he says. 'We are still considered as guests in many, many places. In parts of eastern Europe, even in western Europe, there is a growing anti-Semitism, which the authorities in those countries are doing absolutely nothing to prevent. We are not safe yet.'

For all his defence of a Jewish state, Guy seems prepared to accept that Israel is not, and cannot be, an exclusively Jewish state. Next year, his daughter will go to a school where Muslims and Christians also attend. It's a bilingual school too: she will learn Arabic as well as Hebrew. 'We espouse this view [of a real two-state solution]; now we are going to live it as well.'

C. B. Kaye is also a Dubliner, but he lives in a very different kind of Israel from Guy Gordon or Robert Segal. He lives on a religious kibbutz in northern Israel, not far from the Sea of Galilee, which the Israelis call 'Lake Kinneret'. If you asked C.B., he would tell you that he is a Jew first and an Israeli second. But his desire to live in Israel was born out of his political beliefs; the religious aspect came afterwards.

'I got interested in being a Zionist because my grandfather was in the IRA and fought the British. I thought I would go to Palestine and do the same. It was always my dream to come here,' he remembers. 'In Wesley College in Dublin, I already had the idea of coming over. I was farting my way through school at the time, getting nowhere. A Latin teacher of mine said to me: "Look at you, you big useless lump, sitting there wasting your time, and my time, and your father's money. Why don't you go over there and help your poor people, who are fighting for their existence in Israel."'

This was 1948: Israel had just declared its independence, and the first war with the Arab nations had begun. C.B., who was just fifteen at the time, told his teacher: 'Miss, I want to. I am dying to get out there, but my father won't let me.' Shortly afterwards, his father decided to accept the teacher's appraisal. He took the 'big useless lump' out of school and sent him off to work. 'I just didn't want to study,' C.B. recalls.

C.B. has happy memories of Dublin in the late 1940s and early 1950s, but there were incidents when, as a Jewish family, they felt like outsiders in Catholic Ireland. 'Every so often, I would get into arguments at work,' he says. 'Sometimes I got knocked about on the street. One time, I got chased out through Shankhill in Dublin by a whole gang of fellas calling me a Jew. And I remember saying to myself: Why am I running? I cannot run any more. So I took a branch of a tree and I hit one of the first buggers to come near me and I nearly broke his back with it. On another occasion, I saw my father getting into a fight on a bus after someone told my mother to "Move over, you fucking Jew woman".'

'Ireland was very, very slow to let the Jewish refugees in after the war,' he says. 'Even before the war, there was a possibility of taking people in, but the government would not do it. In fact, there were people working against it. But there were Nazis who came in after the war – helped by the Church, of course.'

The young C.B. joined a Jewish youth group, which sent him to a farm in England to turn him into a suitable volunteer for the Zionists. Unlike a lot of Jews, who became nationalists because of their religion, C.B. came at it the other way round. 'We belonged to an Orthodox church in Dublin,' he says, 'but I was never that religious. When I became involved in the politics of Zionism, I had to take an interest in religion too.'

C.B. is still religious. Kibbutz Lavi, where he has lived most of his life, is an orthodox religious settlement. It started as a collective farm, but its main business now is its hotel, which caters for religious Jews from all over the world.

'When I came over here to stay in 1955, I was twenty-two, and I didn't come with the idea of fighting anybody,' he tells me. 'I thought: there has been a war, and the Arabs will get used to the idea of us being here. Whoever thought that this shit was going to go on until this day?' Like many of the young Jews who went over to Israel from Europe after the War of Independence, C.B. was not told much about the recent history of the land where he was about to settle. The myth of 'a land without people for a people without a land' was very strong in those days.

So he wouldn't have been told how Lavi had been part of an Arab area called Louba, or how more than 3,500 Palestinians had fled or had been driven off their lands in that area. Some ended up in the refugee camps; others were taken by the Israeli army, put on trucks, and transported to new locations within what is now Israel. By the early 1950s, there were only a few Arab villages around the new Jewish settlement.

'I had rocks thrown at me by Arabs here in the Galilee [area], and I had to beat the shit out of people once or twice,' says C.B. 'But apart from that, I was always friendly with the Arabs: I went to Arab villages, and we used to visit their houses. I am a completely open, liberal type of person.'

But what about all the Palestinians who were not rehoused inside Israel but were instead driven off the land to live in the refugee camps? Has he any sympathy for them? 'Unfortunately, the Palestinian refugees were used as a bargaining card by their own people, and they were allowed to remain as refugees,' says C.B. 'It's a very unfortunate situation, but they have been kept that way by the Arab countries and UNWRA [the United Nations Relief and Works Agency for Palestine Refugees in the Near East]. They are the only refugees in the world that are going nowhere. There were many more refugees in India and Pakistan [after Partition in 1947], and they were absorbed. They [the Palestinian refugees] are just a political tool for the Arabs.'

Like all Israelis, C.B. is set against the idea of any full-scale return of the refugees to their former homes. But what about the notion of a symbolic return as a gesture of goodwill? 'If there were only a few thousand, I would not mind,' he says, 'but the Arabs are saying that everyone ever born in a camp is now a refugee, which is just a load of bloody nonsense.'

Is he prepared to make peace if the Palestinians recognise

the State of Israel on the ceasefire lines drawn up after 1948? Would he be willing to give back what Israel captured in 1967? 'Well, maybe,' he answers, then quickly adds: 'But if you ask if half of Jerusalem is up for negotiations, definitely not. It's not theirs. It was never theirs! Look, what would have happened if they had won the war in 1948? Do you think we would be discussing a Jewish state now if that had been the result? Would we be talking about dividing up Jerusalem? We would not!'

If he is prepared to think about handing back the West Bank, does that mean that he would be willing to move out the hundreds of thousands of Jewish settlers living there? 'After what happened a few years ago in Gaza, I don't think so,' he says. 'When we moved the settlers out of Gaza, they [the Arabs] just turned it into waste ground. Are they not going to do the same in the West Bank?'

If they do, isn't that entirely their own business? Shouldn't they at least be given the chance to do something? 'Look,' he says, 'there are twenty-two or twenty-four other Arab countries out there. If they don't like it here, the Palestinians can move out and live in one of them. I have been given a godly right to a large part of this land. My message to the Arabs is: you went to war, and you lost. That's your bloody problem. If you had sat down and made peace then, you would have twice as much as you have now.'

I say that there isn't much point in talking about that now. The question is: what's next? You have around 80 percent of the land, and they have about 20 percent. 'I feel terrible about the situation they are in,' he replies. 'Gaza in particular is desperate, but this is a situation that has been engineered by their own people. If they would spend the money on education and food instead of guns, they would not be in the situation that they are in today.'

Would you like to see a Palestinian state? 'I would not like to see one, but it has to be set up sometime. They have to have their own place. But I would prefer them to go elsewhere.'

I point out to him that Israel is in a strong position. Can it not afford to give something back? He says that Israel is strong 'possibly by virtue of having a strong army', but that the country is weak in the sense that 'groups all over the world [are] trying to put pressure on us'. I ask him what he means by that. 'Well, I mean that, for instance, there are groups in Ireland – and I amazed at this – calling for boycotts of Israeli goods because of what they call an apartheid state here.' At the same time, he says, nothing is being said about 'Sudan or Darfur, or about the terrible things going on anywhere else in the world. If that's not anti-Semitism, then I don't know what is.' Is he hopeful of a peace deal being reached in his lifetime? He starts to laugh. 'Well, I haven't long to go – maybe ten years or so – but it's hard to see it happen by then.'

Despite his pessimism, C.B. says that he has no regrets about leaving Dublin and coming to Israel. He has a wonderful wife, Jenny, four children and ten grandchildren. 'I have taken part in one of the greatest events of the century,' he says. 'Where else has a people come back from five thousand years ago and settled in their own land?' Then he has one last dig at the old country. 'We even revived our ancient language of Hebrew. And where is the Irish language today?' he says with a laugh.

Rabbi Arik Ascherman was recently convicted of a breach of the peace and sentenced to a few weeks' community service. If you were to ask Ascherman, his definition of community service would be to do what he was doing when he was arrested. His crime was obstructing Israeli security forces who were trying to tie a young Arab man to the front of their jeep to 'shield' themselves from stone-throwers during the demolition of an Arab home in East Jerusalem. 'There is this false idea here that if you criticise Israel, you are questioning its legitimacy,' he says.

'I believe the opposite is the case.' During his trial, Ascherman tried to make this point, saying that he did what he did because of his opposition to discrimination against the Arabs, which he describes as 'illegal and immoral'. But the judge refused to hear those arguments.

According to the latest opinion polls, ending the conflict with the Palestinians is not high on the priority list of most Israelis. Corruption in the government is the issue that concerns people more than anything else: 33 percent of those polled gave that as their top priority. Twenty-two percent believe that strengthening the army and dealing with Hezbollah and Iran is the most important thing for Israel's politicians to do. Fifteen percent listed crime as the issue that was most in need of attention. Just 10 percent of Israelis described the Palestinian question as the top priority.

Part of Ascherman's campaign is to make Israelis aware of the injustices that are suffered by the Palestinians. Do Israelis know what is going on in the Palestinian territories or are they being wilfully ignorant? 'Yes, people have hardened their hearts,' says the rabbi, but he adds: 'This is natural when you are being shot at.' According to Ascherman, many Israelis 'downplay what the occupation means for Palestinians. In the same way, Palestinians don't really get what terrorism does to the Israelis.'

This reminds me of the conversations I have had with Israeli soldiers who refused to serve in the occupied territories. The men had complained of being ordered to treat Arabs in an unlawful and immoral manner. They had described being given illegal orders, which resulted in the injury or death of innocent civilians. When I asked them whether they discussed their actions with family or friends, most replied that they didn't, because people didn't want to know, or just didn't care.

For many Israelis, this is a reflection of a core belief that the Arabs are at fault, both for starting the conflict and in failing to end it. 'So many people place no limits on what is permissible in the name of defence and security,' says Ascherman. 'Whatever is requested to provide security is justifiable.' And it goes further than that. 'In a way, some people are even prepared to admit that Israel is violating human rights and breaking international law,' he says, 'but in the name of security it is all justifiable in the end.'

So what happens if you spell out the consequences of that policy and a public attitude that allows it to continue? I quote the figures to Ascherman: Israel has killed about a thousand gunmen and more than two thousand innocent civilians in the current intifada. Could someone describe this as being acceptable? 'Well, if you put it to them that bluntly, they would probably hum and haw and not give you a straight answer,' he replies. 'But it's hard for people to accept these facts because most Israelis really do believe that we have the most moral army in the world.'

I quote another statistic: the 'most moral army in the world' has killed eight hundred children in six years. Is there not a serious question mark over its moral code? The rabbi's answer is this: 'I would say that that is a very serious stain not only on our army but on our country.' He accepts the suggestion that many Israelis are simply in denial about what is being done in their name by the armed forces. 'We have closed ourselves to the pain of others,' he says. 'Israelis have created a bubble around themselves to keep out what they do not want to know.' But to some extent, they are being kept in the dark by their own government. The army is not fully accountable: it does not have to explain the circumstances of the deaths of these innocent people. 'That's true,' says the rabbi. 'It is not acceptable that the resources are not there to investigate every case. And it is also unacceptable that those investigations that do take place are carried out by the army itself. It's the same with the police. They investigate themselves. There should be a system of independent investigations.'

What are the consequences for Israeli society of the lack of accountability of the army? 'The toll is enormous. It is destroying our morals. Almost by any measure it is bad for Israelis,' says Ascherman. 'Both Israelis and Palestinians are convinced they're the victims, and they get outraged if you suggest that they are the victimiser. They don't seem to realise that you can be both at the same time. We Israelis are victims. We have been victims for thousands of years. We have been victimised by the Palestinians and the Arab world. But we are also victimising others. We have abused human rights and we have killed. Both sides have to learn that your victimhood, even if it's real, doesn't give you carte blanche or absolve you when you do wrong.'

Ascherman believes that there is a great deal of confusion on the issue of Israel's responsibility for its Palestinian neighbours because the basic beliefs of both the left and right wing have been eroded. On the right, not many people now believe that a military solution to the conflict is possible; on the left, many people have given up on the notion of exchanging land for peace because there is no one to talk to on the Palestinian side. 'This is what's called the luminal moment,' Ascherman says. 'We are betwixt and between. It is a very dangerous time, because it's when demagogues can appear to offer solutions. But it is also a time of opportunity, because when people are searching for answers it provides space for a leader who can cogently explain how we got here, and how to get out of it.'

Ascherman believes that Israelis have to realise that 'if we don't help ourselves, then no one is going to help us'. He says that, although the overall picture is still pretty bleak, 'I think the most important thing we can do is to break down stereotypes on the other side and give hope'. He is a rabbi, after all: faith and hope are part of his armoury. 'This is not the first time there has been a crisis,' he says. 'And every time, we fight our way back.'

*

'The need to solve the Israeli-Palestinian conflict is as much an existential necessity for Israel's moral health and welfare as it is for the Palestinians national aspirations,' says David Rosen, the former Chief Rabbi of Ireland, and now part of the ecumenical movement based in West Jerusalem.

Rabbi Rosen admits that Israelis have switched off from the Palestinian issue because they are sick and tired of the fighting in Gaza, the Lebanon war, the constant rocket attacks, and the infighting among the Palestinians. But he says that Israelis turn their backs on the Palestinian question at their peril because 'human rights is an indivisible concept, and once you are desensitised in one area you begin to be desensitised in another'.

He says that people block out what is happening because they feel threatened. According to Rabbi Rosen, everyone in this situation see themselves in a different paradigm. The Palestinians feel threatened by Israel, the Israelis feel threatened by the wider Arab world, and the Arab world feels itself threatened by the might of Western power. 'Nobody feels secure,' he says. In Israel, this feeling of fear is combined with an element of aggressive posturing in what is called the 'Pitiful Samson complex'. As Rabbi Rosen puts it: 'On the one hand, we want pity and compassion, but on the other, we want to be seen as powerful and strong.'

For Rabbi Rosen, the creation of a Palestinian state is not just good for the Palestinians, it is good for Israel. 'At the moment, everybody feels that they are weak, and as a result they take positions that actually exacerbate their weakness instead of making them stronger. That's why we need a counsellor from outside to help us through this dysfunctional relationship.'

14

'WE HAVE TO FIGHT TO PREVENT OURSELVES BECOMING LIKE THE NATIVE AMERICANS'

'Are you a Protestant or a Catholic?' the little sheik wanted to know when he heard I was Irish. Discussing my religious background with Ahmad Yassin, the spiritual leader of the Islamic group Hamas, was probably not a good idea. Besides, Yassin was on the Israeli list of targets, and I wanted to get out of his home in Gaza City as quickly as possible.

It had taken two days to line up the interview. When we arrived, the sheik, a paraplegic, was not ready: he was still being washed and dressed by the two young men who gave perpetual care to him. They had solemnly brought in two basins of water and proceeded carefully to bathe his feet and hands, while he sat there motionless, a slight smile on his face. As I watched him, I was thinking about how this man had personally sanctioned suicide bombings against Israeli civilians.

I knew that he would not countenance any argument that this tactic was morally wrong and politically stupid. But I had to ask. His response, as expected, was reflex. He calmly explained that Israel had left the Palestinian people with no choice but to resort to suicide bombings: the Israeli people had to understand that there would be a high price for killing innocent Palestinians. So you accept that the Israelis who are killed are innocent? I ask. A piercing stare. Then a shrug to suggest maybe yes, or maybe no. But are they innocent? I ask again. 'The killing will stop when the Israelis end the occupation,' he responds.

Ahmad Yassin asked about my religious background after the interview, as the crew was packing up. My instinctive response was to tell him to mind his own business, or to tell him that I was an atheist. But I opted to tell him that I was a bit of each: half-Catholic and half-Protestant. I thought that might confuse him long enough for us to be ready to go. 'I think you are more Protestant than Catholic,' he told me. 'Because the Protestants side with the Israelis and the Catholics with the Palestinians, and you have been asking me the questions a Protestant would ask.'

Two weeks later, the Israelis tried to assassinate Yassin by dropping a bomb on the top floor of an apartment building where the Hamas leadership was meeting. But the men were gathered on the ground floor, and Yassin escaped uninjured. The next attempt succeeded. The Israelis waited until they had him literally in their sights. As he left a local mosque after early-morning prayers, they launched several rockets, and killed him. In a bizarre expression of anger, his supporters ran through the streets, chanting his name and waving badly buckled bits of his wheelchair in the air.

Yassin was like all the Hamas leaders in that he was less than forthcoming on the question of what the organisation was fighting for. They always talked about ending the occupation but were vague on the subject of exactly how much land they wished to 'liberate'. The clearest answer any journalist could get from them was a pledge that they would observe a long-term ceasefire with Israel if the Jewish state agreed to pull back to the old 1967 borders. But at the same time, they maintained the position that all of the land occupied by the State of Israel belongs to the Palestinian people.

The answer to that question is still broadly the same: Hamas will agree to a ten-year truce if Israel pulls back to the ceasefire line drawn up after the 1948 war. Beyond that, they will not discuss the possibility of a formal recognition of the State of Israel. As far as the Israelis are concerned, nothing has changed. The Hamas Charter still refers to the goal of the destruction of Israel, and the group has refused to end its armed struggle. They say that they will 'respect' all previous deals between the PLO and Israel but stop short of saying outright that they would be prepared to work those agreements.

But there are some signs of a shift in the Hamas position. In the summer of 2007, Ghazi Hamad, the spokesman for Prime Minister Akram Haniyeh, said that Hamas would 'accept' a Palestinian state on the 1967 borders. Hamad is known to be one of the more moderate, or at least more pragmatic, members of the senior echelons of Hamas.

Hamad answers questions about the group's refusal to end the violence and recognise the State of Israel by trying to change the subject. 'Why are people always imposing preconditions on the Palestinians?' he asks. 'No one is asking Israel to stop the killings. No one is asking Israel to stop building the wall, to stop the assassination of Palestinian leaders, to stop bringing Jews from all over the world to live in the heart of Palestine.'

'We have no country, we have no borders, we have no army,

we have nothing,' he continues. 'And on top of that, you want us to give the Israelis security and recognition, and we have nothing to trade.' The last few words of that answer are seen by some commentators as an indication that Hamas is willing to do some kind of deal – that the organisation is holding out until it feels that it can get some guarantees from the Israelis.

As Hamad puts it: 'The world is not asking the individual members of the Israeli government, do they recognise the right of Palestine to exist? If you do, you would find that some of them would say no, or they would lie. Israel wants recognition from its victims. If we give Israel recognition now, who can give guarantees that anything will change in the near future? The answer is: no one.'

'For Hamas, recognising Israel means to legitimise what Israel has done to the Palestinian people,' explains Diana Bhuttu, a lawyer and former member of the PLO's negotiating team. According to Bhuttu, Hamas cannot bring itself to say that it recognises the State of Israel as long as that fact results in the Palestinians continuing to be deprived of their rights. Perhaps part of the difficulty for Hamas is that it has not decided what kind of movement it is; as a result, it is confused about exactly what it wants. Bhuttu acknowledges that this is a problem. 'Hamas doesn't know whether it is a nationalist movement or an Islamic movement,' she says. 'Before the election, Hamas was everything to everybody. But now it has to define itself.'

Bhuttu is a Canadian-born Palestinian who came to Ramallah in 1996, just three years after the Oslo Accord had been signed, and during a time of some hope. She worked for several summers with the Palestinian human-rights organisa-tion Al Haq and spent some time in community projects at Beir Zeit University, just outside Ramallah. In 2000, she decided to work full time for the Palestinian cause, taking up a position with the legal-affairs department of the negotiations-support unit of the PLO. She has now returned to being a law lecturer at Beir Zeit.

According to Bhuttu, the problem for ordinary Palestinians is that the conflict, and the means of resolving it, has always been defined by someone else. To some extent, she says, that is now changing, and people are becoming better at organising themselves and arguing their case. 'There is now the opportunity [for Palestinians] to define the goals and create a strategy,' says Diana. She believes that this is essential if the Palestinians are to get away from the old strategy of 'just fighting back'. 'Up to now, the Israelis were playing chess and the Palestinians were playing ping-pong,' Bhuttu says. 'They [the Palestinians] were just responding, but the Israelis were three moves ahead.'

So what exactly do the majority of Palestinians actually want? The Palestinian Centre for Policy and Survey Research carries out regular face-to-face interviews with about 1,200 Palestinians at 127 randomly selected locations. The results are collated by Dr Khalil Shikaki, a respected and independent academic. The surveys are supported by the Konrad Adenauer Foundation.

A year after the election of Hamas, and shortly after the formation of the unity administration involving Hamas, Fatah and a number of independents, 48 percent of Palestinians wanted the new Palestinian Authority to recognise the State of Israel, agree to honour all previous agreements between the Palestinian Authority and the Israelis, and end the violence. These are the three conditions which the international community had been demanding that the Palestinians accept. It is also what Israel wants.

True, the same number of people were against their government meeting the conditions. But it was a start. A clear majority of 72 percent of those questioned supported the Arab League plan for an end to the conflict, with a Palestinian state being established in the West Bank, Gaza and East Jerusalem in return for the 'normalisation' of relations between Israel and the twenty-two Arab states.

There was one other significant finding. Seventy-one percent of those polled were in favour of negotiations aimed at an interim settlement which would establish a Palestinian state in the Gaza Strip and in some 80 to 90 percent of the West Bank. This would then be followed by negotiations on the other issues, such as permanent borders, refugees and holy sites. In other words, people were starting to see different ways out of the conflict. And they were trying to negotiate their way out of it, rather than to achieve independence through violence.

But the key to understanding the Palestinian position is the notion that they feel that they cannot accept any further compromises. Part of the fallout from the failed talks in Camp David in 2000 was the feeling among most Palestinians that politics had not delivered. Not only had the negotiations failed to deliver, but they, the Palestinians, were being blamed for that failure. As Bill Clinton's special advisor on the Middle East, Robert Malley, had pointed out: 'In their own eyes, they were the ones who made the principal concessions.'

Malley also put his finger on another important aspect of the Palestinians' approach. 'Most Palestinians were more resigned to the two-state solution than they were willing to embrace it; they were prepared to accept Israel's existence, but not its moral legitimacy,' he wrote. The war for the whole of Palestine was over 'because it had been lost'. Malley rightly pointed out that Oslo, as the Palestinians saw it, was 'not about negotiating peace terms but terms of surrender'.

And he goes on to explain that, given the Palestinians' view that Oslo was the historic compromise where they agreed to giving up 78 percent of mandatory Palestine, they were sensitive to the Israelis' use of language. At Camp David, Israel's claims to be 'offering' land, being 'generous' or 'making concessions' were heaping insult upon injury for the Palestinians. As Malley put it: 'It seemed doubly wrong, in a single stroke both affirming Israel's right and denying the Palestinians.' In other words, for the Palestinians, land was not given but given back.

'Palestinians have always been spoken for by somebody other than themselves,' says Hisham Abdullah, a Palestinian journalist who has been covering this conflict for thirty years, seventeen of those spent working with the AFP news agency. 'If our voices are to be heard outside Palestine, they have always had to go through other filters – mainly the Israelis and the international news outlets.'

The Israeli-Palestinian conflict is the most covered conflict in the world, but that does not mean that the coverage is the most comprehensive in the world. 'There are more journalists permanently here than in any other place bar Washington,' says Hisham, but when he says 'here', he means 'Israel'. 'The majority of them live in Israel, and they see us through Israeli eyes.'

Another problem is that there is little history of independent media in the Palestinian territories. Under Arafat, newspapers and the electronic media were carefully monitored, if not censored. Many of the key editorial staff were politically aligned. This situation has loosened up slightly in the last couple of years, but many Palestinian journalists are slow to push the boundaries of free speech. 'We are not as bad as the other Arab countries, but we are not as good as we should be,' says Hisham. 'There is openness here in the sense that people talk openly. They criticise Arafat and Hamas and whatever else they want to say, but this is not always reflected in the writing.'

The knock-on effect of this situation, he says, is that there has not been a full and open debate about the important issues. One of the most divisive issues for the Palestinians is the fate of refugees. Yet this subject is not being discussed in Palestinian society. Academics and researchers have studied the problem of the refugees, and the PLO has its stated position. An agreed strategy is even more crucial now, given Israel's demand that the Palestinians' claim of a universal 'right of return' be dropped in advance of any negotiations.

Hisham believes that the reality on the ground at the moment would make the creation of a viable contiguous Palestinian state extremely difficult to create, and to maintain. He says that there is a lack of political will, both externally and internally, to make this happen. 'The Israels say they want Abu Mazen as a Palestinian leader, but they have done little or nothing to help him,' he says. 'And that's because they are not really committed to the idea.' Hisham believes that Hamas does not really want a Palestinian state either – or at least not the kind of Palestinian state that the majority of Palestinians want. 'Hamas wants an Islamic territory on as much land as they can control,' he says. 'That's more important for them than a state which is largely secular.'

'This has not been a good year for European democracy,' says Suad Amary, an architect and writer living in Ramallah. 'It has shown how undemocratic and unprincipled the world can be.'

Suad supports neither Fatah nor Hamas but says that 'at the end of the day, Hamas won the elections, and we cannot deny that'. For her, the biggest disappointment was that the West did not object to what she calls 'the reactionary social programme of Hamas and their fundamentalist beliefs'. Instead, the West focused their objections to Hamas on one thing: whether they recognised the State of Israel.

'It appears that if tomorrow Hamas recognises Israel, then it is all right with Europe. It is "end of story" for the West. But for me it is the beginning of the story.' According to Suad, there are still many Palestinians like her who are left without an alternative political leadership. 'If we look at it with a clear head, the support for Hamas is really only about 30 percent of the people,' she says. 'That leaves 70 percent who do not support them, so they are a minority. But they cannot be ignored.'

Suad believes that Europe went along with Ariel Sharon's agenda in undermining Yasser Arafat. She says that she understood why Sharon did it: she believes he wanted to maintain the state of war, in order to continue to confiscate Palestinian land. 'Sharon and those like him have to work to create the conditions where there are no partners for peace on the Palestinian side. First, it was a case of claiming that Arafat was unwilling [to make peace], then the argument became that President Abbas was unable,' she says. 'Now, the Israelis can be seen to be doing something to help Abbas, but that help falls far short of enabling real negotiations over Palestinian statehood.'

Suad believes that this policy of undermining the secular movement resulted in the strengthening of Hamas. 'It's obvious why Sharon did that,' she says, 'but the question is why Europe did nothing to stop it, and even supported that policy.' She thinks that European leaders were perhaps not aware of the possible results of this approach but argues that they should have been. Or that it is a consequence of history. 'Israel always blackmails Europe over its treatment of the Jews during the Second World War,' she says. 'Europe has a guilt complex, and Israel abuses that. The Europeans are hostage to their own history.'

I put it to Suad that part of the problem for the Palestinians is the perception in the outside world that they implicitly support Hamas and its campaign of violent resistance. That sense is strengthened by the lack of any real campaign of non-violent protest against the occupation.

'If we compare ourselves to any occupied people, I am surprised how non-violent we have been' is her reply. 'When people talk about the violence, they are referring to the phenomenon of suicide bombers, which first appeared in 1996. But the occupation has been there since 1948 or 1967.' She believes that most of the resistance has taken the form of non-violent demonstrations, but it is the violence that makes the headlines. 'It is a myth that we have been violent,' she says. She adds that it is up to the Palestinian people to decide whether to use their legal and moral rights to opt for armed resistance to a military occupation by a foreign power. 'It is certainly not up to Israel and America to decide whether we are entitled to take up arms against the invader,' she says. But she is against violent resistance for strategic reasons. 'It is stupid to use violence, because we do not have a chance,' she argues. 'It is far better to opt for non-violence, because we are morally and ethically stronger, and we should not give the Israelis the excuse to do what they do.'

However, she accepts that the public protests against the occupation have dwindled. 'We have reached a point where there is no energy left. There is a small demonstration here and there, but nothing is happening. Every day we get another slap on the face. We have no will to get up and go to the streets.'

'We have not done our homework as to how to fight the Israelis,' she continues. 'At the moment, we do not have a leadership. Abu Mazen is a credible, decent man, but he is not a leader. Nor is Hamas a viable leadership for us. They do not have the necessary skills. In a way, we are worse off than before. In the first intifada, we had no government but we had leaders. Now we have a government but no leaders.'

Suad argues that one of the major problems facing the Palestinians is that they have been 'beheaded politically' and that 'our skills base has completely eroded'. After the Oslo Accords in 1993, tens of thousands of Palestinians returned from America and Europe. They had ideas, energy and money. But slowly, they have been worn down. 'Now they are leaving,' says Suad, 'or they are being refused entry.'

The returned diaspora was the great hope of the Palestinian moderates. 'It's these second-generation Palestinians who have the skills to combat the modern tactics of a First World state like Israel,' says Suad, 'and maybe that's why they are not being allowed in.' She is talking about the thousands of Palestinians who returned to places like Ramallah using foreign passports and three-month visas. For years, they extended their visas to allow them to live and work in the West Bank. Now the Israelis have begun clamping down on these returned emigrants, refusing them visa extensions, or just banning them from living in the Palestinian areas altogether. Queries about the reasons for them not being allowed to stay are met with a single-word answer: 'security'.

The prospects for a fair solution to the Middle East conflict are slim, according to Suad. As she sees it, Israel is setting about imposing a unilateral solution. The State of Israel has finally accepted that there will be a Palestinian state. Even George Bush is saying it. 'So they are thinking that if it is going to happen, they might as well control it,' says Suad. 'That's what the building of the Wall is all about. Israel is defining the final borders of Palestine.'

As far as Suad is concerned, this will produce a terribly unfair outcome which will breed resentment for generations. If the Israelis actually want to resolve the dispute, instead of just ending another chapter in it, they will have to negotiate a fair deal with the Palestinians. 'You can be moral, or you can believe in power, there is nothing in between,' she says. 'The Israelis

have to accept that what they did was wrong. If they accept
this, it does not have to mean the end of the State of Israel. But
retaining a state that was built on the notion that might is right
is immoral, and that is unsustainable.'

Forty-year-old Akram Bakir is one of those Palestinians who
returned to Ramallah to try to build what he hoped was a fledgling state. His mother and father were both born in Jerusalem
but left the city in the 1950s. They went to America and eventually settled in Virginia, where Akram was born. They returned
to Palestine when Akram was fifteen, and he spent the next
seven years in Jerusalem, where he attended secondary school
and college.

After the Oslo Peace Accords, Akram became a spokesman
for Faisal Husseini, the PLO's representative in East Jerusalem.
Then he quit politics and went to live and work in Germany for
ten years. Akram's wife Mariel is an Arab citizen of Israel, but
the State of Israel refuses to recognise his marriage. As a result,
Akrim has to use temporary visas in order to live and work in
Ramallah.

After returning from Germany, Akram worked as a consult-
ant to the governor of the Central Bank of Egypt and as a senior advisor to the governor of the Central Bank of Palestine,
working on the restructuring of the institution. But that was
before the Israelis began proceedings to have him deported.
After being refused free movement into or out of the
Palestinian territories on a number of occasions, Akram lost his
contracts with the banks. Then he spent all of the family's savings paying for a lawyer to fight the expulsion order. Now he
and Mariel struggle to provide for themselves and their three
children, all aged under eight. The Israelis gave no reason for
refusing to issue him with papers to live in the Palestinian territories. He is understandably angry and bitter.

'We have been left in limbo,' says Akram in a soft American accent. 'The Israeli strategy has been very obvious: they will drag it out until I get tired and give up. Thousands of Palestinians who are American citizens are similarly affected. These are business people and investors. They are middle class and educated. They are the people that Palestine needs, and the sort of guys the Israelis need too. But they don't want us here. Instead they want a bunch of bearded guys shooting guns, because they are easier to deal with than some business people who might actually make this place work.'

Akrim and his family lived in Ramallah during the worst of the violence. He never got involved in the violence, and even tried to organise a series of non-violent street demonstrations. Through Israeli peace activists, he and the other organisers of the protests told the Israeli army what they were trying to do. 'We wanted to avoid getting shot,' he laughs, 'so we told the IDF there would be thousands of people on the streets for a peaceful protest.' The group also contacted Hamas leaders to make sure that they ordered the militants to stay away on the day. 'That was another worry,' says Akrim. 'If Hamas gunmen used us as cover for attacks on the Israelis, there could easily be a bloodbath.' Both sides agreed to the organisers' requests.

A week before the protests began, Israeli agents killed Hamas leader Ishmael Abu Shanab in Gaza. The streets erupted with fresh violence; the peace marches were called off.

Akram says that there are different kinds of violence on the Palestinian side. Some of the violence at the grass-roots level was simply the personal frustration of people who had seen loved ones killed and wanted to respond by killing Israelis. But at another level, particularly in the Islamic groups, the attacks were seen as the latest part of a five-hundred-year fight in which the Palestinian fighters were going to outlast the Israelis.

'We never had a viable strategy,' says Akram. 'Armed struggle had its uses in the 1970s and 1980s in waking up the world to what was happening here. That bit worked. But after that, not one piece of Palestinian land was ever liberated by the gun.'

Like many Palestinians, Akram remembers the first intifada in the late 1980s as 'a popular movement where everybody could participate'. But he says that most people either don't want to pick up weapons now or can't do so, and that the current intifada therefore excludes 98 percent of the population. 'This is not a popular uprising in that sense,' he says.

Not surprisingly, he blames the Israelis for escalating the violence. 'On our side, it moved very quickly from stone-throwing to rifles and machine-guns. But the Israelis went from guns, to heavy weapons, to tanks and helicopter gunships. And it somehow became acceptable to use these weapons in Palestinian towns and cities. The first time Israeli tanks went into Jenin, Colin Powell was on the phone to the Israelis asking what was going on. Now, no one bats an eyelid if twenty tanks go into any Palestinian city.'

Akram says that he was always opposed to the suicide bombings. 'Morally, they are wrong,' he says, 'but purely on a tactical level, they are completely counterproductive. If your aim is just to kill as many people as you can, you will never succeed militarily.'

He says that there was never a debate within the broader Palestinian national movement about the use of suicide operations. 'But within Hamas, there was a clear decision to adopt the strategy. It had a lot to do with internal politics. Hamas wanted to show itself as the strongest player on the Palestinian scene. The problem is that this developed a momentum of its own. And the other militant groups followed.'

Does Hamas have a political strategy? Akram thinks that the group is still developing one. 'They made a huge leap in joining the political process,' he says, 'but at the same time, many of them became just another bunch of thugs on the block.' He tells me that he was against the international boycott of the Hamas administration and would favour some kind of reconciliation between the Islamic group and the former ruling party, Fatah. 'Not everyone in Fatah was corrupt and ineffi-cient,' he notes. 'There were a lot of good, honest people who kept the wheels turning.'

So what about Hamas's core beliefs? Is it a religious move-ment or a nationalist organisation? Akram likens the organisa-tion to the left-wing Palestinian revolutionary groups, who believed that they could only liberate Palestine by first over-throwing the corrupt Arab regimes. Similarly, Hamas believes that only the 'Islamic nation' can liberate Palestine, and the group claims membership of that alliance. They believe that a successful Islamic government in Palestine will inspire Islamic movements in places like Egypt and Jordan to take power.

Akram is not sure whether this strategy will work. 'Palestinians in general are not Koran-thumpers,' he says. 'People here are not ultra-religious. We like religion-lite. Hamas have taken prominence because of the misery of the situation. Marx had it right. These guys are offering spiritual opium. The slogan "Islam is the solution" says it all. No explanation of what or how, just a bland statement.'

He believes that it is now too late for a two-state solution. 'I don't believe in it any more,' he says. 'We may need two states as an interim solution, but I don't think there is any alternative to us all living in one country. The settlements are making it such anyhow, and economically, the two cannot survive inde-pendently.'

I suggest to him that that the Israelis would rather die than give up on the idea of a Jewish state. 'That's probably true,' he says, 'but it's also true that Israel, which is a tiny little country, cannot hold out forever. It will be destroyed if it does not come to terms with the region and start to deal with everyone here on equal terms, starting with the Palestinians. The danger is that Israel will be overrun and, in trying to defend itself, will have to kill millions of Arabs. But for them to do that in order to survive would signify the ultimate failure [of the Zionist experiment].'

Akram believes that the notion of a Jewish state is an anachronism, just as an Islamic or a Christian state is an anachronism. 'The Jews are no better and no worse than anyone else,' he says. 'Why should they have a separate state?' I suggest that it is about safety or security. 'Well, if it is about safety for the Jews, then it has failed, because if you look at the way Israel has been constructed and maintained, then the Jewish state is the least safe place for a Jew to live.'

So what about the prospects for peace? Does he believe that the two sides can hammer out a deal? 'If they want to, yes' is his answer. 'But that could take a long, long time. If we want to get it done quickly, we have to involve the Americans. Despite the fact that they have no credibility among the Arabs, they are the only ones with the clout to force a deal in the short term.'

He has given up on George W. Bush but believes that a new US president, such as Barak Obama, could achieve something by acting boldly. 'If the new American president declared that his or her first foreign-policy goal was to hammer out a fair agreement, not just in the first term but in the first six months of the presidency, they could achieve a lot. If the US was to invite the two leaders to Boise, Idaho, for talks, exclude the world's press corps and set a deadline, things could move quickly. If you create that kind of juggernaut, you silence the extremists on both sides. No Palestinian or Israeli leader has the power to say no to the American president.'

'On the Palestinian side, we lack a leadership with a clear-cut vision,' says Jerusalem community leader Terry Balata. 'Normally we know what we want. But now we don't. To be in this position after forty years is a disaster. When we were dying and when we were being put in prison, we knew what we were dying for. This generation does not know what they want.'

As a young woman back in the 1980s, Terry was involved in the mass protests of the first intifada. So were many other Palestinian women. Now things are very different. Terry says that once the gunmen went into the streets, most of the people withdrew. It was not safe to be out there. 'As soon as the leaders became violent, the Israelis were more than ready to respond with violence,' she says. 'Now, we really don't have the leadership that can tell the militants to back off, to get out of the streets and let the people demonstrate.'

Palestinians currently have two governments: Fatah in the West Bank and Hamas in Gaza. 'We are worse off now than we ever have been,' Terry tells me. She believes that even when Fatah and Hamas were part of a national-unity government, they had no common strategy. For her, Mahmoud Abbas lacks the leadership skills to move the situation forward. 'He is too low key to be able to lead people like the Palestinians,' she says.

Hamas leader Ishmael Haniyeh is stronger, but does he have a plan? 'Haniyeh does have a plan,' she says, 'but it is not *his* plan. It's the plan of the more radical external leaders of Hamas, like Khaled Mishal.' Terry thinks that the external Palestinian leadership is influenced too much by the views of the wider Islamic movement, the Muslim Brotherhood. 'It really annoys me that we have been fighting for forty years without much help from Arab countries like Syria and Egypt,' she says, 'and now we are back under their influence because of the links between all those various forces. We need our Arab brothers, but we have our own interests. It is not a true Palestinian position any more.'

Like many Palestinians, Terry is now extremely worried that they are fast approaching a situation where a two-state solution to the conflict with the Israelis will be out of reach for several generations. 'The clock is ticking, and we are in the last fifteen minutes,' she says. 'This is largely because of the facts on the ground. The growth of the settlements, the building of the Wall, and especially the Jewish control over all of Jerusalem.'

On the issue of refugees, Terry wants Israel to acknowledge what it did in creating the situation. 'If they do, then we can sit down and look for a fair solution,' she says. Part of that solution, she maintains, is again down to strong leadership on the Palestinian side. They need someone who will be straight with the refugees. 'We have to be able to say to people that if you want to go back to Haifa, then understand that you will go back as an Israeli citizen and live under Israeli rule. The moment that you bring in the element of reality, then I think many refugees will say: no, I don't want to go back.'

So what needs to be done, in her view, in the fifteen minutes that remain? 'There has to be real international pressure on the Israelis to stop creating these facts on the ground that will eventually make a two-state solution impossible,' she says. 'Even if it is stopped now, it will be difficult. But it's not impossible. If there is something irreversible, like a particular settlement, then we can work out a deal on land exchange, but we need to get some land of equal value elsewhere. She believes that the outside world has to work to encourage this, because failure will mean that what comes out of Palestine in the future will be much worse than Hamas. 'I am talking about the likes of al Qaeda,' she says.

Terry Balata is one of those Palestinians who maintains contacts with the Israeli peace movement. Real dialogue with the Israeli Left is impossible right now. 'I don't know whether it's too soon or too late to talk about the big issues,' she says, 'but we can't go near them at the moment. But what we Palestinians have to do is try to reassure the Israelis that we are not all out to kill them.' She is not hopeful that any real moves towards peace will emerge in the short term. 'This Israeli government doesn't want to find a solution,' she says. 'They are deliberately delaying until they have completed their task of unilaterally drawing the borders.'

So what will happen if that goes ahead? 'The struggle for independence will go on as long as it takes. As long as there are Palestinians here, the fight will go on. A former Israeli prime minister, Ben Gurion, once said of the Palestinians that "The old will die, and the young will forget." Now, sixty years later, the old did die, but the young will never forget, and that is the only hope we have. We have to fight to prevent ourselves becoming like the Native Americans.'

15

'WE'RE RIDING HERD HERE, GUYS'

As *Air Force One* began to circle over the Jordanian port city of
Aqaba, President George W. Bush started to speak to the journalists who had been invited forward for a few quick words.
Down below, on a clearing at the edge of the Red Sea, they
were preparing for the launch of the president's 'Road Map to
Peace'. This was June 2003, and the plan, drawn up by the
Quartet of the United States, the EU, the UN and Russia, was
the deal that was going to end the Palestinian-Israeli conflict
once and for all.

'You know what we're at here?' he asked the press corps.
'What's that, Mr President?' some eager hack asked. 'We're riding herd here, guys. We're riding herd.' A few of the journalists
laughed, but many wondered whether the ersatz cowboy knew
as much about the Middle East as he did about being a ranch-
er. If George W. thought that Yasser Arafat and Ariel Sharon
were a couple of dumb steers to be rounded up and driven in
one direction, he was sadly mistaken.

Arafat wasn't even in Aqaba. The president of the
Palestinian Authority had not been invited. To the Americans,

he was 'no longer a partner for peace'. The only man on the Palestinian side who was powerful enough to make the deal stick had been ordered to stay at home and watch events unfold on television. In his place, came Mahmoud Abbas, better known as Abu Mazen. Abbas, who had appointed as prime minister by Arafat, was an honest man, but he had been given little real power by Arafat.

The Israeli leader Ariel Sharon had already made clear that his acceptance of the Road Map was conditional on the Palestinians meeting their obligations first. Bush shared the view that the process was to be 'sequential' and the Palestinians had to act first in order to prove their good faith. Only then would the Israelis begin to meet their commitments. The Palestinians understood that the two sides would move in parallel, and the Europeans agreed with that reading. The herd was already wandering off in different directions.

But the real question marks were over Bush's own involvement. When he was first elected president in 2000, Bush had made it abundantly clear that he wasn't going to touch the Arab-Israeli conflict. It was the new administration's view that President Clinton's attempt to broker peace just a few months earlier had been a disaster not just for the Palestinians and the Israelis but for American foreign policy in general and the prestige of the presidency in particular.

The events of September 11 changed all that. The White House now saw the Israeli-Palestinian conflict as a contributing factor in 'global terrorism'. The view was that the conflict was being used as an excuse to stoke up the fires of jihad against the West, and the United States had to dampen things down.

But Bush didn't really ride herd. He quickly bounced back to Washington on his buckboard, leaving ranch-hands like Colin Powell, special envoy Anthony Zinni and a few others to whistle in vain as the whole thing descended into a stampede. In the eyes of one close observer, what happened was this: 'President George W. Bush articulated a vision of two states, Israel and Palestine, and he oversaw the formulation of a Road Map for moving towards a realisation of that vision. But there was no sustained US effort or leadership, and no willingness to push both sides to take hard steps. The result was a Road Map to nowhere, and a vision without substance.'

These are the words of Daniel C. Kurtzer, who served as the US ambassador to Israel from 2001 to 2005, the period when all of this was happening. In a piece written for the *Palestine–Israel Journal* in the spring of 2007, Kurtzer admitted that 'American leaders and envoys, it appears, have been unwilling to take the hardest steps towards the peace we say is vital to out national interests.' Mr Kurtzer fears that the United States has 'lost its will and determination to engage in the nitty-gritty work of brokering Middle East peace'.

He believes that Americans have been prone to 'resort to lofty rhetoric and armchair diplomacy' in this area. He gives leaders and officials credit for 'sometimes demonstrating strong emotional commitment and sometimes engaging quite earnestly [with the issues]'. But, he adds, 'We have not shown toughness on the tough issues'.

Kurtzer was not having a go only at George W. Bush. He points out that President Clinton did not engage in Middle East peace efforts until halfway through his second term. When Clinton did get involved, says Kurtzer, he embarked on 'a series of high-profile diplomatic gambits whose failures seeded an already dismal environment, the result of which was bloodshed rather than reconciliation'.

Needless to say, Kurtzer is no longer US ambassador to Israel – or anywhere else. Nor is he likely to be offered another post any time soon. His thirty years of service with the US Foreign Service is now at an end, and he is currently teaching Middle East Affairs at Princeton University's Woodrow Wilson School of Public and International Affairs.

As Kurtzer points out, only the Americans have the power to knock heads together and force some kind of a resolution to the conflict. So why was President Bush unwilling to roll up his sleeves and get stuck in? The short answer is that Bush did nothing because the Israelis wanted him to do nothing. At every turn, Bush was outmanoeuvred by a wily Sharon, who was more intent on consolidating territorial gains than on discussing real concessions.

Sharon made all the right noises. He spoke about ending the occupation. He talked about 'terrorism versus democracy' and all the other generalities that Bush liked to hear. His best move was to take seven thousand settlers out of Gaza and then slip ten thousand more into the West Bank. Gaza was dispensable, but Sharon was intent on holding on to as much of the West Bank as the expansion of settlements and the construction of the Wall would allow. In the end, he even got Bush to articulate Israel's bottom line for any negotiations. In advance of any discussions between the sides, Bush announced that Israel would not be expected to give up any of the main settlement blocs in the West Bank, nor should it have to concede the right of return of the Palestinian refugees who had lost their lands in 1948.

When the fighting broke out again, Bush looked the other way or made vague pronouncements about showing restraint. But it was clear to everyone whose side he was on.

The failure of the American-sponsored Camp David peace talks in 2000 had largely been blamed on the Palestinians. President Clinton, who had brokered the talks, clearly pointed the finger at Arafat. The new White House administration, and the American public, had generally accepted the version of events that says that Clinton set up the possibility of a good deal, Israel played its part by making 'its most generous offer', and the Palestinians responded with yet more violence.

But it wasn't quite like that. Right up to the start of the talks, Yasser Arafat said that he was not ready, and he pleaded with Clinton not to raise expectations, because the mood on the Palestinian street was not one of further compromise. He told Clinton that the Palestinians had already made their big offer at Oslo by agreeing to give up 78 percent of the land and to accept just 22 percent for a Palestinian state. Not a square metre more could be conceded.

Israeli prime minister Ehud Barak didn't seem particularly confident either. He was going for the 'big bang' approach to negotiations: all or nothing. But his fragile coalition was collapsing behind him, the right-wing parties already had one knife in his back, and opposition leader Ariel Sharon was sharpening a few more. Yet Barak seemed determined to go ahead.

Clinton, nearing the end of his second term, dearly wanted a major foreign-policy success. Peace in Northern Ireland would be good, but an Israeli-Palestinian deal would secure his place in history. Whenever the talks threatened to collapse – which was most of the time – Bill was there, like an over-eager teacher at the high-school prom, pushing and cajoling two teenagers who didn't want to dance. Or didn't know how to.

After the Camp David talks collapsed, Clinton managed to bring the two sides back together in Washington in late 2000, and again in Egypt in early 2001. But the Israeli and Palestinian leaders were not directly involved, and although the teams of negotiators did manage to narrow the gap between them, there was nothing like an agreement.

After the talks failed, Clinton sought self-justification by pinning the whole thing on Arafat. The Palestinian leader behaved like the perfect fall guy by not stopping the violence and not explaining his side of the story. Instead, he tried to turn the tap of violence on and off, hoping to gain some leverage for when the talks resumed. But there was little chance of that – and none at all when he finally lost control of the streets.

So the lie that Ehud Barak had made 'the most generous offer' to the Palestinians, and that they had rejected it, was allowed to grow. Barak's offer may have been the most generous offer an Israeli prime minister had ever made, but that doesn't make it generous per se. And it doesn't mean the Palestinians had to accept it. The Palestinian view was that the offer was not from the Israelis but from the Americans, and was therefore not an offer at all.

Barak claimed that Arafat rejected his offer because he wanted 'a Palestinian state in all of Palestine' and that he was saying 'no' to a two-state solution. Barak's conclusion, which many Israelis believed, was that Arafat sought Israel's 'demise'.

But then Robert Malley spoke up. Malley was a special assistant to Bill Clinton on Arab-Israeli affairs and was present throughout the negotiations. In a series of lengthy magazine and newspaper articles, Malley and Palestinian-affairs commentator Hussein Agha laid out a different version of events.

On the assertion that the Palestinians rejected a two-state solution, Malley says that 'the facts do not validate that claim'. In his summary, Malley wrote that 'it is hard to state with confidence how far Barak was actually prepared to go. Had any member of the US peace team been asked to describe Barak's true positions before or even during Camp David, indeed were any asked that question today, they would be hard pressed to answer'.

Malley said that 'the final, and largely unnoticed, consequence of Barak's approach is that, strictly speaking, there never was an Israeli offer. The Israelis always stopped one, if not several, steps short of a proposal. The ideas put forward at Camp David were never stated in writing, but orally conveyed. They generally were presented as US concepts, not Israeli ones; indeed, despite having demanded the opportunity to negotiate face to face with Arafat, Barak refused to hold any substantive meeting with him at Camp David'.

Malley claims that the proposals were not detailed. If they had been written down, he says, the American ideas at Camp David would have covered 'no more than a few pages'. Barak and the Americans insisted that Arafat accept the proposals as general 'bases for negotiations' before launching into 'more rigorous negotiations'.

According to those 'bases', Palestine would have sovereignty over 91 percent of the West Bank; Israel would annexe 9 percent of the West Bank and, in exchange, Palestine would have sovereignty over parts of pre-1967 Israel equivalent to 1 percent of the West Bank, but with no indication of where either of these portions of territory would be. On the highly sensitive issue of refugees, the proposal spoke only of a 'satisfactory solution'. Even on Jerusalem, where the most detail was provided, many blanks remained to be filled in. Arafat was told that Palestine would have sovereignty over the Muslim and Christian quarters of the Old City, but only a loosely defined 'permanent custodianship' over Haram Al Sharif, the third-holiest site in Islam. The status of the rest of the city would fluctuate between Palestinian sovereignty and functional autonomy. Finally, Barak was careful not to accept anything. His statements about positions he could support were conditional, couched as a willingness to negotiate on the basis of the US proposals so long as Arafat did the same.

The failure of Camp David was significant because it altered the perception of the Palestinians in general and Yasser Arafat in particular. Arafat the Nobel Peace Prize winner was now painted as the man who had wasted a historic opportunity. Once the violence escalated, Arafat was only a short slide away from being described as a terrorist. Ariel Sharon, who replaced Barak as prime minister, was only too happy to goad Arafat into playing that role. Sharon blamed Arafat and the Palestinian Authority for every attack carried out by the various militant groups. The Palestinians tried to explain that if Israel, with all its military manpower, could not stop the bombers getting in to Israel, how could the Palestinian security forces stop them getting out of Palestine? But Sharon wasn't in the mood for listening. He had already ordered the army to hit back hard and to target the infrastructure of the Palestinian Authority. The more he did this, the less inclined the Palestinian security forces were to rein in the militants. In the end, they just threw away their uniforms and joined them.

While all this was going on, the newly elected George W. Bush was trying to distance himself from the conflict. Much of the killing might have been avoided, and some of the irreparable damage to the peace process avoided, had Bush stepped in quickly and ordered an immediate truce. However, by the time he got took an interest, the ferocious nature of the fighting meant that neither side was interested in a truce, let alone a peace process. What little trust had existed was gone. The Israeli public, most of whom had supported Barak's attempts to negotiate a two-state solution, threw up their hands in despair. They quickly went from being extremely wary of Arafat to despising him. The Palestinians were equally incensed. As they saw it, Barak had tried to humiliate them, and now Sharon was exposing the true face of Israeli intentions.

By allowing Sharon to act as freely as he did, Bush proved to the Palestinians, and to the wider Arab world, that he was not to be trusted. As Bush's acquiescence developed into outright support for Israeli policy, the Palestinians increasingly saw America as more than just a dishonest broker. They saw the US as the enemy too. It was at about this point that Bush was trying to launch his own peace process.

When that process unravelled, as it was bound to, the Bush administration reverted to a hands-off policy. Even after Arafat died and Abbas replaced him as Palestinian Authority president, Bush failed to seize the initiative and take real steps to strengthen Abbas. There were handshakes and handouts, of course, but Bush always stopped well short of doing something substantial, because that would have meant putting pressure on the Israelis. Abbas had also taken over Arafat's position as leader of Fatah, the ruling party. Had he received real support from the Americans, Abbas, and by extension Fatah, would probably not have suffered such a setback in the subsequent elections as they did. But many people saw him as weak and ineffectual, and they voted for Hamas in droves.

When that happened, Bush took another step back. The Americans now had the perfect excuse for ditching the peace process. Instead, they cut the aid to the Palestinians and backed Israel's refusal to talk to Hamas. But as Ephraim Halevy, the former head of Israel's Mossad secret service, pointed out, this conflict is 'the only one where the US is still maintaining an ideological approach'. Halevy argues that if the Americans are prepared to engage in direct negotiations with the North Koreans, and to sit at the table in Baghdad with Iran and Syria, then why not talk to Hamas too? No one is asking Israel to begin talks on a Palestinian state with Hamas, just to find out what they are looking for. If it's out of the question from Israel's point of view, then that's the end of that.

And as Halevy also reminds the Americans, it was they who insisted that the Palestinian elections to go ahead with the inclusion of Hamas. The Israelis wanted to lock up every Hamas candidate as soon as his or her name appeared on the ballot paper. In the end, Israel waited until after the voting, and then rounded up most of the newly elected Hamas cabinet. And both they and the Americans began talking to Abbas in an attempt to maintain the fiction that he was the one in power and that they were interested in a peace process.

But Abbas had no power other than the power of the security forces, which were loyal to Fatah. When Hamas tried to take that power away, the fighting erupted. As soon as things reached a point where President Abbas felt compelled to dissolve the government and appoint an emergency cabinet,

America was back in the game. The US promised financial support for Abbas and even revealed that it had previously been urging the President to collapse the government. Among Hamas supporters, this was further evidence that Abbas was succumbing to the pressures – or the charms – of the United States.

But all of this is just tinkering around the edges. It seems that America will do nothing except continue to support Abbas and, in doing so, strengthen the perception among many Palestinians that Abbas is collaborating with an American administration that firmly backs Israel.

It appears that there is no willingness on the part of the Americans to deal with the causes of the conflict, and so they allow it to continue. The approach is one of conflict management, not conflict resolution. The US and EU maintain what they think is a kind of status quo by giving billions of dollars to Israel and billions of euro to the Palestinians. As the Americans try to manage the conflict, the Europeans try to manage the humanitarian crisis. But the latter stems directly from the former, and in a sense Europe is just throwing money at the problem.

The simple fact is that there is never a status quo in this conflict. The situation worsens because the cause of the problem, the apparatus of occupation, has become a serious obstacle to any efforts to persuade the Palestinians to adopt a common political strategy. The Palestinians are too busy dealing with the effects of the occupation to work out how to end it. Meanwhile, the US and the EU behave as if there is no occupation. They ignore the land seizures, the building of the Wall, the house demolitions, and the hundreds of violations of basic human rights, and now approach this problem as if it was a land dispute between two equals.

*

The Europeans don't really care how the Palestinians use their money providing it's not for guns. The Americans, on the other hand, don't mind what the Israelis do with their money provided that they *do* buy guns. American guns. In February 2007, the Bush administration asked Congress for $2.4 billion for Israel's 'security needs'. This was the largest sum ever requested under the current deal between the two countries. Israel used to get $3 billion a year in total, of which $1.2 billion was to buy American weapons. Then came an adjustment, whereby $120 million would be cut from the overall grant each year but an additional $60 million would be added to the security budget.

Israel negotiated a special deal during the recession of 2003 to get $1 billion in special military aid and $9 billion in loan guarantees. On top of all this military aid is the money for 'civilian' purposes. How Israel spends that is its own business.

The American government's generosity is such that in 2005, Israel felt able to ask it for $1.2 billion in special grants to help relocate the settlers who were being uprooted from Gaza. But the proposals were shelved after Hurricane Katrina, when the Bush administration had to find money to help displaced Americans instead.

With Hamas in power, the United States froze all direct aid to the Palestinian Authority. But it was providing weapons for the Fatah-led security forces, controlled by the 'moderate' President Abbas. The Americans say that they are anxious to avoid a civil war between Hamas and Fatah. But just in case it happens, they obviously want to ensure that the outcome is to their liking. The fact that their support for the Fatah forces is exacerbating the tensions seems to have been missed. Or it was deemed an acceptable price to pay. But many Palestinians believe that the US wanted a conflict because they felt that Fatah could then take full control and crush Hamas. In Gaza at least, they badly misread the situation, and helped create the deep schism that has now emerged.

Meanwhile, the Americans and Israelis managed to get Europe to go along with the demand that Hamas meet their three key demands before anyone dealt with them. The condition which caused Hamas most difficulty was that they immediately recognise the State of Israel.

Hamas view withholding recognition of Israel as one of their few bargaining chips, and they are unlikely to give it up without something in return. But they also believe that Israel's demand for recognition is merely a ploy to prevent talks and that, even if the demand is met, it will be quickly replaced with another one. According to Halevy, the demand for recognition is 'superfluous'. He says that the other demands – that Hamas ratify all previous agreements and prevent militant attacks on Israel – are both 'reasonable and imperative'. But the American ideological approach of insisting on a boycott until recognition is given is 'politically unwise and inefficient in practice', he says.

Opinion polls suggest that most Americans either broadly support their government's action in this conflict or simply don't know what to think. American-born anthropologist Jeff Halper is heads of the West Jerusalem-based Committee Against House Demolitions. As its name suggests, the group began by trying prevent Palestinian homes from being bull-dozed, but it has since developed into a group lobbying on a range of issues. When I spoke to Halper, he was just back from a speaking tour of the United States. 'Americans have either been getting no information or just a one-sided view,' he says. 'After nine-eleven and the Palestinian use of suicide bombings, it became very difficult to get information across to ordinary Americans.'

Halper is solidly left wing. He is also an Israeli citizen and a Jew. 'Self-hating Jew', 'Arab-lover' and 'traitor' are some of the more polite terms of abuse he suffers. I ask him whether the

Americans are not worried about the backlash if this conflict goes on. 'Sure they are,' he replies, 'but they appear to have a different method of dealing with the problem. Look, last year the Pentagon issued its twenty-year work plan, which it calls the "Long War". Basically, this says that the West is in a twenty-year generational war with radical Islam. There is a commitment for $1.4 trillion of new weapons systems in the pipeline for the next two decades. So there is obviously a tremendous commitment to the idea of this long war.'

According to Halper, the American logic is not to accommodate the Muslim world but to beat it. Therefore it will not get involved in this conflict other than to support Israel, which, in that scheme of things, is fighting radical Islam, in the shape of Hamas and Hezbollah. The 'war on terror' scenario makes Israel's close military alliance with America crucial for the latter. 'Israel is tremendously useful militarily. It's very much involved in the American military-industrial complex in terms of weapons development,' says Halper. 'Overall, Israel's uses, in terms of the long war, outweigh the negative effects of the fight with the Palestinians.'

Catherine Cook is a senior analyst and media coordinator for the Washington-based Middle East Research and Information Project. She is an American, and has been living in Ramallah on and off for the past decade. She doesn't believe that a change in the White House in 2008 will necessarily prompt any great shift in American policy, even if a Democrat becomes president. She says that the two parties have almost-identical policies on this issue. 'My sense is that the only reason they are engaged [in the Middle East] at all is that they think that, if they can make some progress, or at least seem to be interested, it will deflect any criticism of their wider policies in the Middle East.'

Cook is not convinced that US policy in relation to the region is hugely influenced by the power of the pro-Israel lobby. 'I think they [the Americans] act the way they do because they don't always understand what's going on,' she reasons. 'I'm not sure there's an independent analysis. A lot of the time it appears that the Bush administration is simply getting the read from Israel. Of course it acts in its own self-interest, but it sees that self-interest as acting in the interests of its ally in the region.'

Cook thinks that the American-inspired Road Map to Peace plan was essentially doomed from the outset because 'there was no workable deadline, in fact the deadline had already passed a month before the plan was released'. She argues that the whole thing collapsed because it was premised on the 'time-line theory', according to which progress could be made only if certain deadlines were met. One of the conditions was that the Palestinians maintain calm in the occupied territories for a certain period of time, and 'that was never going to happen'.

In fact, it could have. At around the time of the launch of the Road Map, Hamas leader Abdel Aziz Rantisi offered a truce in which the Palestinians would end its attacks on Israeli civilians if the IDF stopped killing Palestinian civilians. Sharon rejected the offer, insisting that there would be no deal with Hamas and that it was up to the Palestinian Authority to disarm Hamas. Two weeks later, two Israeli helicopter gunships fired several missiles at Rantisi's car in Gaza, missing him but killing two people and injuring twenty. A year later, after several other planned attempts, they finally killed him.

Following the failure of the Road Map, Catherine Cook sees that 'the tendency now in the United States is to push for a permanent-status agreement immediately'. According to Cook, the Americans and the Israelis see that the Palestinians are greatly weakened by the last seven years of the conflict, and the danger now is that the Palestinians 'will be pushed into accepting a plan which creates a kind of a state with provisional borders and some kind of a formalised, interim agreement which is actually permanent'. She believes that a Palestinian entity created on that basis would be unworkable.

In early 2007, in a poll conducted by the Zionist Organisation of America, 60 percent of respondents said Israel should not 'give more land to the Palestinians'; 11 percent said they should. The use of the word 'more' is a little strange in this context, since Israel has never ceded full control of any land to the Palestinians.

When asked 'Do you think a Palestinian state would be a terrorist state rather than a peaceful democracy?', 45 percent said 'yes', while 22 percent said 'no'. Zionist Organisation of America head Morton Klein, commenting on the findings, said: 'It is not surprising. It's not like the Palestinians are acting like decent people, promoting peace. They're not.'

The American public is naturally more sympathetic towards the Israelis than towards the Palestinians. It's the Judaic-Christian alliance, in which the Israelis are seen to be part of the civilised Western world, whereas the Palestinians are not. According to this simplistic view, the Palestinians voted for a fundamentalist government and are potential terrorists who launch suicide-bomb attacks similar to September 11, whereas Israel is a democracy with a regular army. An Israeli government spokesman once told me that the government had two different kinds of message for European and American audiences. If it was Europe, they stressed the peace process, because Europeans 'didn't really understand' terrorism. When they spoke to the American audience, the emphasis was on 'terrorism', and the background language was specifically geared towards Middle America. 'What can we do if our kids can't go to the mall on a Saturday night for a pizza slice?' was the type of question the spokesperson would ask on CNN or Fox News.

As many Americans see it, this is also a fight between Israel and the Arabs, not merely Israel and the Palestinians. If the conflict is placed in this framework, then Israel is the underdog, seeking a 'tiny strip of land' in a continent of Arab states. That eclipses the image of a State of Israel which has 80 percent of the land and maintains military rule over the other 20 percent and the people who live there.

Catherine Cook agrees that the average American does not know or care about what is going on in the West Bank. But she says that many of those who take an interest in the region may get a one-sided view from the American media. This situation will change only when the Arabs make their voices heard. At the moment, the Arabs don't have a proper political lobby group in the United States, and many of them don't even register to vote. 'They were just beginning to get politicised when 9/11 happened,' she notes, 'and now they don't want to appear on the radar. People are afraid that if they speak up, they will be seen as terrorists.'

According to the online version of the *Economist* magazine, the Arab-American organisations, while increasing in political power, still lack any real clout. They have the potential support of around 3.5 million people but garner only a fraction of that. The magazine reported that between 1990 and 2004, Arab-Americans donated just over $750,000 to various candidates and parties. During the same period, pro-Israeli groups donated almost $57 million.

The Arab-Americans' political organisations have a number of causes to fight, not least the treatment of Arabs in the United States itself, so they are unable to concentrate their resources on the issue of Palestine. Even within the Arab-American lobby, there are differences over the best approach to take, and the desired outcome. According to the *Economist*, religion too is a feature of the divide, with Christians making up 63 percent of the membership of this lobby, and Muslims 24 percent.

*

'The Jews don't control the world, that's just a crock of shit,' says Akram Bakir, an advisor to Faisal Husseini when the latter was the Palestinian Authority's representative in Jerusalem. Bakir left politics to become a banker in Europe and then returned to try to help Palestinian businesses get started after Oslo. But he can't resist still being a political commentator.

'What certain influential members of the Jewish community in the US are adept at is the leverage of power, and we have to harness our resources to counter that,' he says. For Bakir, the failure of the Arab states to finance a pro-Palestine campaign is yet more evidence of the neglect of their so-called 'Arab brothers'. 'Jewish money would be a mere drop in the bucket if the Arabs coughed up,' he says.

The main reason that Arab states like Saudi Arabia won't help, according to Bakir, is that 'Those oil-rich Arab nations are run by illegitimate leaders who help mainly themselves. And they're threatened by the idea of modern democratic, secular Palestine, which is what the majority of Palestinians are fighting for'. Bakir says that the conflict is useful for those Arab states because it is a diversion from their own problems. Will they ever really help the Palestinians? 'Not if it costs them anything,' says Bakir.

There are a growing number of left-wing Jewish groups, including Americans for Peace Now and the Israel Policy Forum, but the largest and most powerful lobby organisation in the US is still the right-wing American Israel Public Affairs Committee. At the organisation's last annual conference in Washington, more than 6,000 delegates turned up to hear speakers like Nancy Pelosi and John Boehner from the House of Representatives and Senators Harry Reid and Mitch

McConnell. Vice President Dick Cheney was also there to deliver a speech entitled 'The US and Israel: United We Stand'.

Yet the image of the Jews in America as right-wing Republicans is simply incorrect. Eighty-seven percent of Jews voted for the Democrats in 2006, all but four of the Jews in Congress are Democrats, and 87 percent of Jewish voters think that the war in Iraq was a mistake. These are not the kind of people who would necessarily support a right-wing government in Israel. In fact, they are the people the Palestinian lobby should be talking to – providing they have something useful to say, and someone to say it.

16

WHAT CAN THE EU DO?

The EU and Israel have a peculiar relationship. Many of the European countries, Ireland included, were slow to allow Israel to join their family of nations. For a long time, diplomatic relations were strained, and trade between European nations and the State of Israel were practically non-existent. Now, trade is good, and through the EU-Israel Trade Association Agreement, Israel enjoys the privileges of being an honorary member of the club.

Israel is also developing stronger cultural links with Europe. Despite not being part of the continent, its soccer teams compete in UEFA's competitions, and it has a place in the European group of the World Cup competition. The country even competes in the Eurovision Song Contest.

The governments may be warming towards each other, but it is still a strained relationship. In general, the Israeli public is deeply ambivalent towards Europe: they like the place, but they are very suspicious of the politics. Many Israelis think that the Europeans are, by and large, hopelessly biased towards the Palestinians. In their view, Europe is either extremely naive or wilfully stupid in giving the Palestinians the support they do, particularly in the form of financial aid. As far as they are concerned, Europe is still a little soft on terrorism and needs fully to wake up to the threat of Islamic extremism.

History teaches the Israelis to be cautious. Europe is where the Holocaust occurred; Europe knew what was going on but failed to act. Israelis frequently mention the lack of support in many parts of Europe for the creation of a Jewish state following the war. They also cite the refusal of many countries, including Ireland, to offer sanctuary to the hundreds of thousands of Jewish refugees who fled post-Nazi Europe. And it is a common belief that anti-Semitism is alive and growing in Europe, and involves more than neo-Nazi skinheads smashing up synagogues on a Saturday night. Many Jews believe that the growing criticism of Israel is prompted by Europe's deep-rooted anti-Semitism.

But at the same time, a majority of Israeli citizens want Israel to be part of the EU. In a survey carried out for the Konrad Adenauer Foundation in the spring of 2007, three-quarters of respondents supported the Jewish state joining the EU. A third of that number expressed 'strong' support for the idea, and only 18 percent of those questioned were against it.

Twenty percent of those aged between eighteen and thirty said that they would move to Europe if they were given the chance. Among the ten-to-nineteen-year-old age group, 37 percent said that they would go if they could. Most new citizens of Israel keep their old EU passports, but recently the embassies of European countries in Israel have reported an upsurge in applications from the children and even grandchildren of people born in EU countries, including the countries that joined the Union recently.

So what can Europe do to help end the conflict? The former Israeli prime minister, Ariel Sharon, neatly summed up his country's view of Europe's role when he said: 'They are payers, not players.'

It's true. In terms of converting financial clout into political influence, Europe is getting significantly less of a bang for its buck than it could. But trade between Israel and the EU is growing, and Europe is attempting to squeeze in at the top table by means of 'constructive engagement' with Israel.

Europe now has financial leverage. Israel is a member of the European Neighbourhood Policy programme: not quite a member of the EU family, more like the potential son-in-law who gets invited to Sunday dinner. The EU has had an Association Agreement on free trade with Israel since 2000, and trade between the two countries is up by about 4 percent each year.

Thirty percent of Israel's exports now go to the European Union, and 40 percent of the country's imports come from the EU. The European Investment Bank has offered €275 million in loans for small and medium-size businesses and environmental projects in Israel. In fact, Europe is so keen to have Israel at the table that the country is now eligible for financial assistance of €14 million over the next seven years. It's not a huge sum, but it's a start.

At the same time as increasing trade, the EU is trying slowly to draw in the Israelis politically, in the hope of having a quiet word in their ear. But this situation is a long way off, and in the meantime Europe is restricted to making soothing sounds and desisting from speaking its mind for fear of frightening off its new friends.

As far as Europe is concerned, the Jewish settlements in the West Bank are illegal, the route of the Wall is illegal, extrajudicial killings are obviously illegal, and the collective punishment of an entire population through the use of hundreds of checkpoints is illegal. So what does the EU actually say to Israel about all of this?

Very little. European governments, and the EU as a body, do not even seem to consider imposing financial penalties on Israel with the aim of forcing them to end the criminal excesses of the occupation. And we could do it. The European Neighbourhood policy is not just about making lots of money for all concerned. It is also there to 'offer cooperation on a wide range of issues, including terrorism, education, health, culture and human rights'. The Trade Association Agreement specifically places a burden on Israel to 'respect human rights and democratic principles'. This is not a polite request but a demand.

Enough members of the European Parliament felt that Israel was not meeting its obligations to call for a suspension of the deal in 2002. Ireland's all-party foreign-affairs committee called for the agreement to be reviewed. But 'review' can be a polite term for looking at something and doing nothing. The EU insists that it lets the Israelis know of its displeasure; diplomacy is, by its nature, something that is done quietly. If the softly-softly approach is not working, then it may be time to apply some firm pressure. But the EU's twenty-seven member states have to agree on what to do.

'The EU is too busy waving carrots and doesn't want to wield the big stick,' says Charles Shamas, chairman of the Ramallah-based human-rights organisation, the Mattin Group. According to Shamas, a Lebanese-American, the danger with the current softly-softly approach is that the EU is setting precedents which may make it impossible for them to turn around later and say to the Israelis: now we want you to do this or that.

'The EU has this fantasy that by buttering up Israel, it will obtain a greater role for itself and so become a key player in the region, including being the ones to broker a peace deal,' says Shamas. 'Quite frankly, instead of Israel moving closer to the EU, in terms of how it operates, it is Israel that is saying to the EU, come closer to me and play by my rules.'

Shamas gives a couple of examples of how difficult it is to get Europe to take a firm stand on Israel's actions. It says that the settlements are illegal under international law but does nothing about them. After the route of the Wall was adjudged by the International Court of Justice in The Hague to be illegal, Europe did nothing. In fact, it could not bring itself unanimously to back a proposal to send the case to the Court in the first place. Several European countries actually opposed the hearings on the basis that this was a 'political issue'. Maybe it was, but that doesn't mean that it can't be a legal issue too.

Even when it came to minor issues, like stopping goods produced in the illegal settlements from benefiting from the free-trade deal, it took the European Commission five years to implement the rules. (Those settlement-produced goods are still imported into Europe, by the way: they just don't get the tax breaks any more.) It was Shamas and his Mattin Group which first highlighted the fact that the Israelis were sending EU countries products made in the settlements. According to Shamas, Israel was simply branding all its export goods 'Made in Israel', and the EU wasn't bothering to check. The abuse wasn't hard to identify. Because it didn't feel that it was doing anything wrong, Israel didn't conceal the fact that these goods had been made in the settlements.

Only after much prodding by various human-rights groups did the European Commission feel compelled to act. The Commission and the Israelis eventually estimated that the value of the goods that were being illegally exported to Europe was about €150 million to €200 million per year. But Shamas and others think that the real figure was far higher, because it didn't take into account the goods that were produced in the settlements and were then transported into Israel before being exported.

After this issue was first raised, there followed a series of notes and memoranda, communications, investigations, reports, inquiries and every other known method of people-talking-quite-a-bit-but-doing-absolutely-nothing. After years of wheeling and dealing, a system was finally put in place to separate the settlement products from the other imports, and to apply the normal customs duties to them. The Israeli government pays the settlement producers a subsidy to cover this additional cost.

But Shamas is not finished with the fight yet. He is investigating whether the export to the EU of settlement goods can be stopped altogether on the basis that there is a crime involved in their production. 'The extensive appropriation of property by an occupying power, unjustified by military necessity, which is the case for all Jewish settlements in the West Bank, is an international criminal act under the Geneva Convention,' according to Shamas. 'When factors of production that have been criminally obtained, or the proceeds of a criminal act, are used in trade, then most member states have their own legislation to stop it.'

Shamas argues that it is up to individual states to decide whether to use this legislation. He is hoping that some will at least look at the possibility of doing so. In strictly legal terms, he says, the question is whether by trading in goods which are known to be the produce of an illegal settlement, 'the importer is therefore implicated in an illegal act'.

Each time the Israeli army blows up Palestinian roads and power stations in the West Bank and Gaza, it costs the European taxpayer a great deal of money. After the setting up of the Palestinian Authority in 1993, the EU began pumping billions of euro into the Palestinian territories. Much of this went on day-to-day spending but large sums were also spent on infrastructure. Some money came from central EU funds, but there were also regular donations by individual governments, including Ireland's.

When the fighting started, much of the infrastructure was bombed to rubble. The EU engaged IMG, the International Management Group, to see how much it would cost to replace it all. At the beginning of 2006, IMG estimated that more than €200 million would have to be spent repairing or replacing property damage that had been directly caused by the Israeli army. Some 1,300 projects were listed in that category. Another 3,500 projects had been badly damaged indirectly, and these required a further €750 million to repair or replace. This was just the running total as of January 2006. Millions of euro worth of further damage has been caused by the Israeli army since then.

In most cases, the attacks on infrastructure cannot be justified militarily. For instance, in June 2006, after Palestinian militants abducted an IDF tank gunner and took him to Gaza, the Israeli air force bombed one of the main electricity stations in the Strip, leaving hundreds of thousands of people with only intermittent power, or none at all.

If the aim was to recover the abducted soldier, the rationale was difficult to understand. Surely it would be more difficult to find him in the dark? Similarly, the decision to destroy some of the main roads linking Gaza City with the rest of the Strip merely ensured that the militants, if they wished to move their hostage, would be forced to use back roads and dirt tracks, making them more difficult to catch. The only other possible motive for the attacks was revenge. The military campaign amounted to the inflicting of collective punishment, which is outlawed under the Geneva Convention.

According to Shamas, Israel, as the occupying power, already bears the responsibility for the costs of any legitimate military action involved in enforcing the occupation. But he says that wanton destruction is different in that it is illegal. 'It's an issue of criminal responsibility,' he says. Shamas argues that the law is clear on what is justifiable and what is not. 'Most of the destruction of EU-funded infrastructure was illegal because it was not collateral damage,' he says. 'It was deliberate, and therefore a violation of the rules of war.'

At one point, the EU examined the possibility of pursuing the Israelis for the cost of repairing the infrastructure. But ownership of the projects had been handed over to the Palestinian Authority, and so technically it was they and not the EU who had suffered the loss. The chances of the Palestinian Authority mounting a case against the Israelis are slim to none. The Israelis have enacted laws to protect themselves from any claims by the Palestinian Authority, or even Palestinian individuals. Besides, if the Palestinian Authority attempted to serve a writ on the government of Israel, they would be quickly hit by a counter-suit.

If Europe doesn't want the Palestinian territories to collapse economically, it must simply grin and bear the cost of continuing to rebuild the roads and the ports, and any other vital pieces of infrastructure that the Israelis decide to bomb. What it could do would be to retain ownership of these pieces of infranstructure, and simply lease the projects to the Palestinians for a nominal sum. Then, perhaps, there might be a legal case for pursing the Israelis for costs and damages.

But Shamas believes that Europe will do nothing which will damage its growing relationship with the Israelis. 'Europe has come to accept the horrible situation of crisis management,' he says. 'They do their humanitarian relief, because not to do it would propel things in the other direction.' He says that the Israelis have effectively manoeuvred the EU into a position where it now effectively underwrites the cost of the occupation and allows the Jewish state to spend its own money on expanding the illegal settlements or building the Wall.

Alvaro De Soto, a Peruvian diplomat and the former UN envoy to the Middle East, has some strong things to say about the international community's apparent subservience to Israel. De Soto spent the last two of his twenty-five years with the UN in Jerusalem. After he quit, he sent a confidential end-of-mission report to his bosses, in which he complained bitterly about the UN's attitude towards Israel.

In the report, which was subsequently leaked, he claimed that the UN had 'put a premium on good relations with the US and improving the UN's relationship with Israel' and said that the UN Secretary General should 'seriously reconsider' the UN's membership of the Quartet, because it had become a 'side show' and 'pretty much a group of friends of the UN'.

De Soto went on strongly to criticise the Americans for what he called 'the tendency among policymakers to cower before any hint of Israeli displeasures and to pander shamelessly before Israeli-linked audiences'. The former envoy attacked Hamas for advocating the destruction of Israel, but he also criticised the UN restrictions which prevented him from holding talks with Hamas or with the Syrians. He also said that Israel's policies seemed 'perversely designed to encourage the continued action by Palestinian militants'. The UN, he added, was not doing Israel any favours by 'not speaking frankly to it about its failings regarding the peace process'.

De Soto's report made clear his opposition to the sanctions that had been imposed on the Palestinians by the members of the Quartet after the election of Hamas. The move had had 'devastating consequences' for the Palestinians. 'The steps taken by the internationalcommunity with the presumed purpose of bringing about a Palestinian entity that will live in peace with its neighbour Israel have had precisely the opposite effect,' he wrote.

De Soto wrote this is in May 2007. A month later, his warning of 'devastating consequences' for the Palestinians were borne out when Gaza erupted in internecine fighting. The clashes between Fatah and Hamas was not just a simple power struggle between two groups. Years of frustration and anger, compounded by the crushing weight of the sanctions, contributed in no small way to the eruption of violence.

The EU's policy of trying to boycott Hamas into submission was doomed to failure from the start. If the aim was to force Hamas to tear up its manifesto and plead to the West for forgiveness, it failed. Instead, it drove Hamas into the outstretched hands of the Iranians, and Prime Minister Haniyeh returned to Gaza with literally a suitcase full of cash. The West responded by trying to strengthen the Fatah end of the national-unity government with money and weapons. To Hamas, this was proof that the so-called 'moderates' of Fatah were intent on a policy of capitulation in the face of bad faith on the part of Israel, bias from America, and lily-livered neglect from Europe.

After the collapse of the national unity administration, Europe again sided with Mahmoud Abbas, despite the fact that Hamas was the democratically elected government. Instead of trying to force Hamas and Fatah to begin negotiations on a truce, the EU helped to widen the gulf by backing Abbas in his decision to appoint an emergency cabinet of his own. This was the American and Israeli agenda, and the EU once again slid quickly into a supporting role, with promises of yet more money for Fatah. Europe attempted to put a gloss on the deal by pledging that the people of Gaza, which was now under complete Hamas control, would not be excluded from the aid. But the government that the had elected was being excluded, and this is what the Palestinians will remember.

Once again the EU was falling into line with the Americans by trying to bully the Palestinians into behaving as the US demanded and punishing them when they failed to meet the grade. At the same time, the Israelis were included as a partner in the enterprise, rather than as the principal cause of the conflict. If the Europeans and the Americans could bring themselves to offer the Palestinians a genuine political horizon, rather than just vague pronouncements of a two-state solution, it would be easier to defuse the tension and undermine the extremists. But to do that, the international community would have to confront Israel. And it won't.

The EU is playing a dangerous game, according to Shawan Jabarin, director-general of the Ramallah-based human-rights organisation Al Haq, which is partly funded by the Irish government. He says that the Europeans know all about the extent of the abuses of human rights in the occupied territories but that they weigh their relationship with the Americans and the Israelis, on the one side, against their respect for international law on the other.

'For them, it is easy to preach about principles and obligations,' he tells me. 'But they do not do anything. Because they serve their own short-term interests, they are not ready to act in pursuit of their obligations. They are afraid of losing money either through the US or with Israel. I don't know if it is a real fear, but it appears to be what they believe.' He thinks that there are serious consequences for the credibility of the EU project.

'Protection of the people is the cornerstone of international law,' he says 'If that is gone, then what is there?'

But what could Europe do if it had the courage of its stated convictions? 'It can do a lot,' says Jabarin. 'They can put economic pressure on Israel. Instead of allowing the Israelis to gain benefit from its relationship with the EU and at the same time to maintain its occupation, they could threaten their privileges.'

According to Jabarin, the real danger lies in the fact that 'Europe is sending a clear message to the outside world that they do not care about truth and justice'. He says that a growing number of Palestinians see Europe now as 'mere followers of the US in terms of their foreign policy'. He accepts that, in reality, there is a difference between some EU countries and others but that 'In the end none of them say no to the US regarding their policy in this conflict. Sometimes they drop words here and there, but they are not prepared to stand behind their words.'

Jabarin says that many Palestinians are now 'losing hope in the international community and in international law'. He says that if this happens, 'The people will take their own ways to protect themselves. If there is nobody to protect them, they will find other, more radical, ways. They will become more fundamentalist.'

He points to the current intifada. 'We have to ask ourselves why most of the people supported the suicide bombers. It is not enough to say it is a horrible practice. That's OK, I agree with that, but you have to really examine why they carried out these attacks. It was desperation. They lost hope in the outside world. The people who did this are not crazy, and the ones who try to say they are crazy try not to answer the questions. They are trying to escape from the answers.'

Jabarin says that the Palestinians are a tolerant people generally but that there are signs that this tolerance is being eroded. 'Maybe next time you will find that Al Qaeda are the ones who are directing the operations,' he says. 'The same is true of the Muslim population in Europe, which is watching closely what is going on here. Globalisation doesn't just mean international trade, it means terrorism too, and the European countries have to be aware that everything they do – or don't do – here will have an impact back home.'

There was a time when being European conferred a kind of special status in the Palestinian territories, or at the very least a level of protection. Not any more. In places like Gaza, which has always been more radical than the West Bank, the feeling towards Europe is increasingly one of hostility. I noticed this first while covering the funeral of Sheik Ahmad Yassin, the spiritual leader of Hamas, who was killed by Israeli forces in 2003. In the confusion of the funeral, I got separated from the local freelance TV crew, and within minutes an angry crowd had surrounded me.

A man who claimed to be a teacher began to cross-examine me about Western media bias. Why was I not telling the truth about what was happening in Palestine? he asked. Why did I not tell people in Europe about the occupation? I told him that the people of Ireland were well informed on the issue. 'Occupation?' he said, beginning to raise his voice. 'What do you know about occupation?'

I talked my way out of the situation by giving him the angry Irishman's drunken spiel about the eight hundred years of occupation and oppression we had suffered under the British. They all shook my hand and wished me well, but I knew that a taboo in Palestinian society was disappearing. Strangers were no longer universally welcome. No longer did everyone auto-matically assume that a European was there to help them, or at least was sympathetic towards them.

*

Dubliner Eoin Murray, who worked with the Palestinian Centre for Human Rights in Gaza for two years and now works for the aid agency Trócaire, believes that 'The real change in how people viewed Europe happened with the imposition of sanctions.' According to Murray, people went out and voted in the elections in huge numbers, but when the EU 'didn't like the results, they punished ordinary Palestinians'. Murray thinks that the impact of this action is being felt right across the Arab world. 'In a single act,' he says, 'the EU destroyed their carefully cultivated reputation. It was take a lot of work to restore that.'

In the years that followed, European aid workers and journalists were the targets of kidnapping by gangs. Irishman John Ging, the head of the UN Works and Relief Agency, narrowly escaped being abducted when the convoy in which he was travelling was attacked and shot at. Sure, these gangs were criminals who had no affiliation with the main militant groups, but the clan that was responsible for the kidnapping of Scottish journalist Alan Johnston of the BBC called itself 'The Army of Islam' and reportedly had links with one of the more radical Islamic groups from outside Palestine.

The majority of Palestinians proclaimed themselves against these kinds of actions, and there were many street protests, but the fact that the groups were able to carry out the abductions might suggest that somebody somewhere knew something and wasn't saying. Either it was a level of tactical support or fear, or both, but either way it highlighted the general collapse of law and order in parts of the Palestinian territories. And this despite the fact that a powerful and well-organised militant group like Hamas was nominally in charge.

Eoin regards the attacks on foreigners as symptomatic of the general collapse of law and order in the Palestinian territories. As he sees it, this is the result of a number of factors. The West's apparent willingness to allow Israel to break international law is a large part of it. But so too is the American invasion of Iraq and the widespread human-rights abuses in neighbouring Arab states, many of which are supported by the West. 'How else do we expect the Palestinians to view the rule of law?' he asks. At the same time as all of this was happening, the Palestinian Authority was being massively undermined both internally and externally.

'Of course criminals and warlords are going to fill the vacuum,' says Murray. 'What's surprising is that it took so long.' The worry now is that the vacuum is about to filled by more radical militant groups, who will try to make the Palestinian struggle part of the global jihad against the West. To date, the Palestinian militant groups, even Hamas, have been careful to keep their fighting directed against Israel. In fact, Hamas has been castigated on a number of occasions by Al Qaeda leaders for having allied itself with the secular Fatah movement in the government of national unity.

However, recent events in Lebanon, where Islamic fundamentalist groups have been recruiting people in the Palestinian refugee camps, have proven that there is an audience of young men willing to listen to the gospel of hate against the West and to join the radical Islamist movement. Rumours persist that Al Qaeda are already there on the ground in Gaza and in West Bank cities such as Jenin and Tulkarem, gathering support and awaiting their opportunity to claim ownership of the struggle. Many of these reports come from shadowy figures in the Israeli intelligence community, who have their own scaremongering agenda to pursue. But there is no reason to doubt that if Al Qaeda are not already active in these areas, they soon will be, and that they will have little problem convincing an increasingly radical Palestinian youth that a global jihad is the best way to pursue their cause. If and when this takes hold, Europeans will no longer have a degree of immunity. They will be targets, not just in the Palestinian territories, but at home too.

CONCLUSION

In June 2007, Tony Blair set out upon what appeared like a fool's errand. George W. Bush had appointed him as the Quartet's peace envoy to the Middle East, but then limited his powers to such an extent that it appeared that little or nothing would actually happen. But the situation could be read the other way: that something big was about to happen, something so big that Bush and Blair were afraid to talk about it for fear of frightening the horses.

Initially at least, Blair's mission was confined to finding out whether the Arabs were ready to do business. They talked about re-establishing the institutions of the Palestinian authority. They talked about the police, and the courts, and the importance of not stealing lots of money from the EU. But Tony Blair had to have a bigger brief than that. Hadn't he? Surely the former Prime Minister of Great Britain and Northern Ireland was not going to risk the same shifting sands that had sucked down Bill Clinton and George Mitchell if the job could be handled by a half-decent diplomat from the Foreign Office.

Surely Blair was really going in there to look the Palestinians in the eye and ask them whether they were ready to make a deal with the Israelis. The Palestinians were no doubt assuring him that they had been ready to do for quite some time. If the plan was what they said it was, Blair would then take the temperature and report back to Bush and the Quartet of interested parties, which represents just about everyone who has a finger – old or new – in the pie. Waiting for the US, the EU, the UN and the Russians to decide what to do next could take some time.

In the meantime, someone had to sit the Israelis down, look them in the eye, and make an informed decision about their preparedness to end the sixty-year war. That is the big question. Because nothing moves until we know where Israel wishes to draw a blue line on the map and reveal the final boundaries of the Jewish state. It appears that Tony Blair is not to know this just yet. Two weeks into his new job, Blair let it be known that he rather hoped to pop in on the Israelis while he was in Jerusalem. The Israelis, with their usual directness, let it be known that they would be away that week. Israel would prefer to talk to George Bush. If you are tiny Israel and you are being asked to make 'painful compromises', you will want something in return. So you do the deal with the most powerful man in the world.

The Israelis know that Bush is the best friend they have ever had in the White House, even if they are also well aware that he has his own agenda. They are not so sure of Blair. His smiley, back-slapping style does not go down well in Israel. It makes them uncomfortable and suspicious. They are not fooled by Bush's ranch-hand slouch either. But he's the sugar daddy who hands them $2 billion for military spending on an annual basis. And another billion for day-to-day expenses. The other problem is that Blair still has a foot in the British and European camps. 'GW' might have been the man who hired him, but Blair has a point to prove at home.

The Englishman would like to demonstrate that not every Middle East adventure has to turn out like the bloodbath that is Baghdad. Blair also knows that, if he even appears to draw conclusions that favour the Bush agenda, whatever that may be, he will come under fire from his former European partners, who would relish the opportunity to take him down. Or at least slow him down. That's if the Russians don't veto the plan first.

What is Bush planning? He has recently been showing signs of becoming reengaged with the Arab-Israeli conflict after several years of seeming not to be noticing what's going on. He and Secretary of State Rice have been saying the right things again: about how there has to be a Palestinian state. But there were also some new hints about the Israelis getting used to living with the territory they had, and not thinking about building Jewish-only enclaves right across the West Bank as far as Jordan. The message to the Israelis seemed to be that it is nearing time to decide where to draw that line on the map. Bush appears to believe that there is a chance that he will be able to force through a deal while the Palestinians are weak and divided, and the Israelis are anxious to get this out of the way so that they can concentrate on getting ready for the Iranians.

Which explains Bush's interest. He wants his buddy Israel fighting fit in case Tehran gets too twitchy. After a long campaign in Iraq, the American forces will need all the help they can get from their only real ally in the Middle East.

So the timing for this latest initiative on the Israeli-Palestinian conflict may be quite good. It's true that both the Israelis and the Palestinians want an end to the conflict. On the face of it, there are enough people on both sides who appear to support a deal to make it a possibility. But the problem is that there is little real appetite for risk-taking. Seven years of bitter fighting has created enough fear and loathing to obscure any path to peace. For the Israelis, Hamas is the personification of all that they despise about the Palestinians: fundamentalists determined to destroy the Jewish state. If Israel's ambitions are unclear, so too is the bottom line for Hamas. What is the least amount of territory that Hamas will accept for a Palestinian state, and what are they prepared to do to get it? It has to begin with what they are prepared to say about Israel. Then it moves on to what they have to say *to* Israel. But the Israelis will not be sitting down with Hamas any time soon, and the Islamic group will have to be heard by someone else first.

But the West is not really listening to the Islamic group. The international community turned its back on Hamas almost immediately after it won the elections in early 2006. If he is to get anywhere, Tony Blair will have to listen. He has been hearing the whispers emanating from the secret diplomatic back channels in Gaza. These suggest that Hamas is prepared to be pragmatic. But the word from the Israelis is that Hamas is rearming and reorganising, and preparing for an upsurge of violence. As the British did with the IRA, Blair will be asking the hardliners for signs of goodwill and honourable intent.

If the British acknowledge that such signs exist, they will slowly inch open the door to the inevitable direct talks between the mediators and the gunmen. Hamas were seen to be giving such a signal when the kidnapped BBC journalist Alan Johnston was freed due to an intervention by the Islamic group. Hamas took their time in flexing their muscles and having Johnston freed. The Hamas military machine overran the Fatah-controlled Palestinian Authority security forces in just three days, but it took them three months to free Johnston from the clutches of a small criminal clan. Why so long? Were they waiting to see what credit they would get in return? After Johnston's ordeal had ended, the British foreign secretary,

David Miliband, went on television and said thank you to Hamas. A few weeks later, the Israeli press thought they detected a softening of the British attitude over the demand that Hamas recognise the right to exist of the State of Israel in advance of any diplomatic thaw.

Though there are many people in the Israeli government who will never trust Hamas and will never make life easy for them, they are not the ones who are really blocking progress. The pressure to keep Hamas hemmed in is coming from the element in Israel which believes that the Islamic group might be serious about a peace deal and doesn't want them to make that transition. They don't want the conflict to end just yet. If they can keep it going, while managing it in such a way as to keep the casualties low, this will facilitate their ambitions of further territorial conquests in the West Bank and East Jerusalem. The longer they can delay the fateful day when Israel has to declare formally its final borders, the more time they will have to expand that domain by grabbing another West Bank hilltop or buying up another piece of Arab land near the Old City of Jerusalem.

Tony Blair will not be dealing with the Israeli hardliners. If he has read his brief, he will know that this is a waste of time. The only ones who can talk to the extreme Right, secular or religious, are the Israelis who are prepared to sign a deal. If an agreement is to be made, Israel will have to move tens of thousands of settlers out of the West Bank. And for that to happen, Israelis will have to demonstrate that there is a large majority in favour of this course of action. It could come to a referendum on pulling out of most of the occupied territories. But that needs an Israeli prime minister who is courageous enough – and strong enough – to call the vote.

Meanwhile, Palestinians will have to make their voices heard too. And this is another reason why Hamas will have to be brought in from the cold. There can be no election or referendum, through which the people of Palestine can express their view, unless the question is asked in Gaza as well as in the West Bank. And that cannot happen while Hamas, which rules over Gaza by popular demand, is excluded from power. The only way that this can work is with Hamas inside the tent.

Before he had his recent bitter falling out with Hamas, President Abbas was pleading with Israel to reveal its idea of a political horizon. This was to give the Palestinian people some hope, but also to bait Hamas into showing their hand. Or at least to make them curious enough to stick their head inside the tent to see what was going on. Before the collapse of the so-called 'unity' Palestinian administration, Hamas had declared that Abbas was free to test the political waters and then report back to the parliament about what was on offer. That leeway appears to be gone, with Hamas seriously worried that Abbas is going to cut a deal with Israel and the Americans that will leave them permanently isolated.

But even if they like Abbas, Israel has ruled out any 'early' talks on the substantive issues of borders and Jerusalem and has tried to keep the question of refugees off the official agenda completely. This 'exclusion order' pared the agenda down to issues such as how Israel could give the Palestinians millions of dollars in tax revenues seized by Israel, release a couple of hundred of the tens of thousands of Palestinian prisoners in Israeli jails, and remove a dozen or so of the hundreds of checkpoints which divide up the West Bank.

The talks did include 'security cooperation' between Fatah and the Israelis – a dangerous strategy for Abbas, who risks being seen as a collaborator. Meanwhile, the goodwill gestures would not include any release of Hamas prisoners, even the parliamentarians, who are left to languish in prison until they soften their stance or at least stop supporting violent resistance in any way.

*

It could be that George Bush is really telling Israel that it has to make compromises. And Israel is ready to make these compromises. Maybe Bush thinks that the Palestinians are in no position to refuse whatever the Israelis offer and that, as a result, this would be a good time to launch a drive for a deal. To sweeten the pill, Europe, the US and other countries will be there to promise the Palestinians billions of euro for reconstruction. On top of that, the Arab League, led by the so-called 'moderate' Arab countries, including Saudi Arabia and other oil-producing states, will pledge large piles of cash for the Palestinians to rebuild their collapsed economy.

If all of that happens, a deal can still be done. But there will have to be a lot of honest talking before we get to that stage. Firstly, both sides will have to agree *among themselves* what it is that they want. Only then can the Israelis and Palestinians begin talking to each other again.

Acknowledgement

The lyrics from John Lee Hooker, 'This World', from *Boogie Chillun*, © 1962 Cireco Music (BMI), copyright renewed, are reproduced courtesy of Concord Music Group, Inc. All rights reserved. Used by permission.